DIVINE THERAPY

&

ADDICTION

DIVINE THERAPY & ADDICTION

Centering Prayer and the Twelve Steps

Based on Interviews with
Father Thomas Keating, OCSO

Interviewer: Tom S.

*The greatest gift that can come to
anybody is a Spiritual Awakening.*

—Bill W., The AA Grapevine,
December 1957

LANTERN BOOKS • NEW YORK

A Division of Booklight Inc.

2009
Lantern Books
128 Second Place, Garden Suite
Brooklyn, NY 11231

Printed in the United States of America

Library of Congress Cataloging-in-Publication Data

Keating, Thomas.
 Divine therapy & addiction : contemplation and the twelve steps
/ based on interviews with Thomas Keating ; interviewer, Tom S.
    p. cm.
 ISBN-13: 978-1-59056-144-7 (alk. paper)
 ISBN-10: 1-59056-144-9 (alk. paper)
 1. Alcoholics Anonymous. 2. Twelve-step programs.
3. Twelve-step programs—Religious aspects—Christianity.
4. Contemplation. I. S., Tom, 1929– II. Title.
III. Title: Divine therapy and addiction.
 HV5278.A78K36 2009
 616.86'06—dc22

                                        2009015275

Cover design: William Jens Jensen

CONTENTS

Part 1: Interviews with Father Thomas Keating,
    OCSO, on the Twelve Steps, 2000–2008

Part 2: Doing the Steps in Depth

*Information in Appendix A, B, and C supports
statements made in both Part One and Part Two.*

BIOGRAPHIES

My name is Tom and I'm an alcoholic. I was born in 1929 and my sobriety date is October 5, 1978. This book is a result of a series of interviews with Reverend Thomas Keating, OCSO, a Trappist monk who is largely responsible for showing me the difference between spirituality and religion and how to intuitively live the principles of the Twelve Steps.

I pray that the words of Father Thomas will help us reach new depths in the healing of our spiritual lives.

Father Keating is a Cistercian (Trappist) monk at St. Benedict's Monastery in Snowmass, Colorado. He was one of the founders of the centering prayer movement and an organization called Contemplative Outreach, Ltd. In 1983, he invited spiritual leaders from virtually all the world's great wisdom traditions for dialogue on their commonality, which continues after 25 years. He has worked with Twelve Step groups, offering centering prayer as part of the eleventh step practice. He is well-known for his numerous books, tapes, and teachings.

AUTHOR'S NOTE

This book came out of interviews conducted for a series of videos on centering prayer and AA. The interview questions are not meant to be all-inclusive. Many came to mind shortly before or during each interview. If, after reading this book, you have a burning desire to ask Father Keating a question relating to the steps or Lectio, please send your questions to: Tom S., c/o Contemplative Outreach Ltd., 10 Park Place, 2nd Floor, Suite 2B, Butler, New Jersey 07405. Perhaps the accumulation of these questions could form the basis for a final interview with Father Thomas.

The Twelve Steps are reprinted with permission of Alcoholics Anonymous World Services, Inc. ("AAWS"). Permission to reprint the Twelve Steps does not mean that AAWS has reviewed or approved the contents of this publication, or that AAWS necessarily agrees with the views expressed herein. AA is a program of recovery from alcoholism only—use of the Twelve Steps in connection with programs and activities which are patterned after AA, but which address other problems, or in any other non-AA context, does not imply otherwise. Additionally, while AA is a spiritual program, AA is not a religious program. Thus, AA is not affiliated or allied with any sect, denomination, or specific religious belief.

Many thanks for the encouragement and support from Bob C., Vince C., my sponsor Buddy K., and the love and support of my family and friends in Contemplative Outreach and AA.

—Tom S.

Centering Prayer in Prison

Write to Contemplative Outreach at the above address for a free copy of *Locked Up and Free*, a simple booklet for men and women who are incarcerated and seek a deeper relationship with their Higher Power.

PART I

*Interviews with Father
Thomas Keating, OCSO,
on the Twelve Steps,
2000–2008*

STEP ONE

We admitted that we were powerless over alcohol, that our lives had become unmanageable.

Tom S.: Good morning, Father Thomas. My name is Tom S. and I am a member of Alcoholics Anonymous. In keeping with the AA tradition of anonymity, I'll be off camera for this filming. We meet again at St. Benedict's Monastery in Snowmass, Colorado, and we must thank Abbot Joseph Boyle for permitting us to use these monastery grounds for today's interview. In my humble opinion, two of the greatest spiritual leaders of the twentieth century were Bill Wilson, an alcoholic and co-founder of AA, and yourself, a Trappist priest, former Abbot, and one of the founders of Contemplative Outreach. You both have written books that enjoy immense popularity, in particular *Alcoholics Anonymous* by Bill Wilson, which was published in 1939, and your two books of recent vintage, *Invitation to Love* and *Open Mind, Open Heart*. Also, you both have basically defined the spiritual journey for all of us as a movement from self-centeredness to God-centeredness. Bill Wilson describes the alcoholic as self-centered in the extreme.

You seem to complement each other in the spiritual realm. One of Bill Wilson's key attitudes in his journey is willingness, which seems to relate to the title of your book *Open Mind, Open Heart*. Bill's main resource for the spiritual journey is the Twelve Steps while yours is centering prayer. A growing percentage of us in AA use centering prayer to accomplish the meditation requirement in the eleventh step. We'll postpone a full discussion of centering prayer for now, but Father Thomas, would you agree with this short definition of centering prayer? That it is a disciplined meditation practice designed to reduce the obstacles to our spiritual awakening, to use Bill Wilson's words. (See Appendix B—An Eleventh Step Prayer Practice.)

Thomas Keating: I can accept that. It covers many of the points that are involved in the centering prayer method.

TS: I always liked that term "spiritual awakening." I think it fits so well with your teachings. Chapter 5 of *Alcoholics Anonymous*, which AA members fondly call the "Big Book," contains a list of the Twelve Steps that Bill Wilson and early AA members took to achieve sobriety. Our main topic today will be step one, which reads, "We admitted that we were powerless over alcohol, that our lives had become unmanageable." Father Thomas, as we read this step, what thoughts or comments from your perspective rise to the surface?

TK: This is a very basic statement. It really is the basic psychological step that has to be taken for any serious spiritual progress. Among the world religions, one is visually inspired by some religious figure, some particular belief in God, or some aspect of religious practice. Although God is not mentioned in the first step, the term occurs further on in the steps. Those who try to initiate a serious spiritual program are going to experience their inability to overcome their old habits or compulsions no matter how much they want to.

This first step highlights the fact that all human beings are deeply wounded. From earliest childhood we start out on the path to self-consciousness without any idea of what happiness actually is, apart from the gratification of our instinctual needs for survival and security, affection and esteem and approval, and power and control. These attitudes are essential to survive early childhood. If the child didn't have the motive for living that these instinctual needs provide, he or she would just roll over and die. But human nature being what it is, and the world being a hazardous place, we can't count on the fulfillment of our instinctual needs, and some children are terribly deprived in one or all of these three areas. Everyone, of course, is deprived in some degree because no parents are perfect, and, even if they are, they can't control the environment, teachers, and important others that enter the child's life. So this poor little creature may feel isolated in a potentially hostile world. It needs lots of love including concrete holding, touching, embracing, kissing, and cooing in order to have a stable emotional life to deal with the ups and downs of everyday life, and to establish a meaningful relationship with God.

So we approach this adventure coming from no self-consciousness to increasing awareness of sense objects, of other people and ourselves. The socialization period from about four to eight greatly complexifies our growing attachment to the gratification of our emotional programs that have become energy centers around which our thoughts, feelings, and desires circulate like planets around the sun. The point I am trying to make is that growing self-consciousness is an addictive process and, as a result, one is on a journey that can't possibly work. In addition to trying to find gratification in those three emotional needs, is added an over-identification with the group one belongs to, whether family, ethnicity, race, community, village, tribe, country, or even religion. The developing global village is going to create a whole new set of relational problems.

In any case, the child has identified happiness for which it's innately programmed with the gratification of the emotional programs and the sense of belonging to a group. At the same time, the child is learning that it can't control people and events as much as it would like to; that it will not receive the broad approval that it longs to have; and that it can't count on survival and security because of the hazards of the human condition such as disease, danger of death, rejection, oppression, or being part of a society that is exploited or downtrodden. These hazards can greatly increase the sense of rejection and the frustration of those programs with which the child has completely identified. The child may also be inclined to them through temperament, genetic inheritance, or number on the enneagram. Other factors in the equation are its parental situation, social conditioning, biological inheritance, and the attitudes of its companions when it learns how to talk. In some cases, genetic factors make certain people more vulnerable to alcohol. They experience a need to use alcohol in order to relieve the pain caused by the lack of gratification of the instinctual needs as these become fantastic and impossible to realize. The child doesn't have the use of reason in its first few years to moderate desires, so it has no way to distinguish what is realistic or possible in its desires for control, affection, esteem and approval, and security. The child tends to want a boundless amount of gratification in every area. When it enjoys occasional gratification, it experiences self-exaltation, pride, self-inflation; and if it suffers frustration, which is most of the time, it experiences the automatic afflictive emotions that go off when an experience is perceived as unpleasant. It's confronted every day with situations that frustrate its desires. Perhaps 90 percent of its desires, psychologists say, are unconscious; in other words, many of our deepest commitments to symbols of security, power, and affection in the culture are rooted in desires that are absolutely impossible to achieve. Actually, every other human being is trying to do the same impossible thing: to try to find boundless happiness in very limited goods. When you're in competition with six-and-a-half billion other people, it just doesn't work.

The human condition has been explained by certain religions as a fall from a higher state. All the world religions have perceived that this is the human condition as it actually is, and that it is virtually helpless to do much about escaping from this program that leads to frequent, if not habitual, frustration. As the pain of frustration increases, it becomes necessary for the psyche to repress traumatic experiences into the unconscious, where their negative energy remains and is warehoused in the body. Everybody is vulnerable to constant frustration. This is why the religions of the world suggest disciplines to reduce the amount of energy we put into one or all of the emotional programs, as well as over-identification with our group that seeks their approval even at the price of our own integrity. In this sense, everybody is either in recovery or on the way to developing an actual addiction. This may also be why many folks in the Twelve Step program who have achieved some recovery still have serious problems and may either develop another addiction or fall back into the one that they've struggled so hard to escape. The spiritual practice that is not only suggested, but outlined and transmitted through the Twelve Steps, is a real path to freedom from the compulsions of the addictive process that may have eventually led them to the addiction of alcohol.

As you know, many people have found the Twelve Steps helpful for other addictions. Alcoholics Anonymous has contributed to society a clear set of principles that describes exactly what the problem is and a path out of it. It is not just refraining from alcohol; it also addresses the deep emotional problems that were the source of the addiction in the first place. *Emotional sobriety* is the term Bill W. uses for a mature Twelve Stepper, one who is beginning to translate the Twelve Steps into the spiritual experience of liberation. The emotional causes and attachments that set off the original addiction are now released so that there won't be another addiction to replace it or another fall from sobriety.

Those words of the first step are extremely powerful. Would you mind saying them again?

TS: Sure. *"We admitted we were powerless over alcohol. . . . "*

TK: Stop there for a second . . .

TS: Okay.

TK: To be powerless means to be absolutely helpless. In other words, you can't do anything under your own steam, will power, or any amount of strategy. You're hooked, overwhelmed, wiped out. This, oddly enough, is the best disposition for the beginning of a spiritual journey. Why is that? Because the deeper one's awareness of one's powerlessness and the more desperate, the more willing one is to reach out for help. This help is offered in the next two steps. You turn yourself over to a Higher Power who you believe can heal you and work with you in the long journey of dismantling the emotional programs for happiness. They are the root causes of all our problems. We try to squeeze gratification or satisfaction out of the symbols of those three emotional programs in the culture to which we belong. Every advertisement addresses one of those three programs, because that's what people are interested in and that's what they'll buy into. Once in a while there is a reference in an ad designed to appeal to one's over-identification with one's group. In any case, these are the two pillars of the false self, the self that we think we are and that wants to find happiness in the emotional programs that can't possibly work.

Please read the second half of the first step.

TS: Yes. *". . . that our lives had become unmanageable."*

TK: This is the logical conclusion of being powerless over some kind of human activity into which we keep falling because we are powerless to resist. The movement of freedom is to let go not only of the harmful substance, but of the kind of behavior that we are powerless to control and which may be damaging to other people or ourselves. As that weakness spreads and involves the whole of our life, it messes up our relationship with God, with other people, ourselves, and the environment. Everything is subjected to our desperate attempt to find happiness through these emotional programs and so the vicious cycle begins. The negative energies that we've repressed and their consequent pain call for some kind of compensation or relief. We then return to that kind of conduct in the past that brought us temporary relief or forgetfulness of the problem. Then we have to find relief from the pain of our addiction and we get more discouraged. This cycle reinforces our need to get away from the pain because the pain keeps increasing as we recycle the pattern. Hence, it's obvious to see why in AA the community is so important; we are powerless over ourselves. Since we don't have immediate awareness of the Higher Power and how it works, we need to be constantly reminded of our commitment to freedom and liberation. The old patterns are so seductive that as they go off, they set off the association of ideas and the desire to give in to our addiction with an enormous force that we can't handle. The renewal of defeat often leads to despair. At the same time, it's a source of hope for those who have a spiritual view of the process. Because it reminds us that we have to renew once again our total dependence on the Higher Power. This is not just a notional acknowledgment of our need. We feel it from the very depths of our being. Something in us causes our whole being to cry out, "Help!" That's when the steps begin to work. And that, I might add, is when the spiritual journey begins to work. A lot of activities that people in that category regard as spiritual are not communicating to them experientially their profound dependence on the grace of God to go anywhere with their spiritual practices or observances. That's why religious practice can be so ineffective. *The real spiritual journey depends on our acknowledging the unmanageability of our lives.* The love of God or the Higher Power is what heals us. Nobody becomes a full human being without love. It brings to life people who are most damaged. The steps are really an engagement in an ever-deepening relationship with God. Divine love picks us up when we sincerely believe nobody else will. We then begin to experience freedom, peace, calm, equanimity, and liberation from cravings for what we have come to know are damaging—cravings that cannot bring happiness, but at best only momentary relief that makes the real problem worse.

TS: In his essay on step one [in *Twelve Steps and Twelve Traditions*], Bill writes, "Only through utter defeat are we able to take our first steps toward liberation and strength." You may have touched on that, Father, in your sharing, but please comment on that concept of "utter defeat."

TK: The repetition of defeat, of trying to overcome an addiction and then falling back into it, is a very difficult experience to deal with. The same applies to practices of the spiritual journey even without an addiction. The addictive process is constantly urging the same pernicious doctrine that if only we can find some relief for the pain, boredom, and struggle of dealing with the particular tendencies that we are trying to correct. Powerlessness, then, is the result of frequent defeat. It has a very dark side, which can tend to lead to despair, which prompts people to seek compensatory kinds of behavior when the pain becomes too great to handle.

On the other hand, from a spiritual point of view, hitting bottom turns us over to complete dependence on the Higher Power. This disposition is the radical foundation on which to build a program of recovery. The healing that takes place is totally gratuitous. Whatever efforts we put into it, prompted by grace, are liberating, not our efforts by themselves. Perhaps you can see the enormous tension that is building up between constant defeat and the tendency to despair, and the inspiration to turn ourselves over completely to God. This disposition is reflected in the words of the Gos-

pel of Jesus Christ in the saying, "I have come to save that
which is lost." The word "lost" means totally gone, hopeless,
not worth giving another thought to, wiped out.

This applies equally to those on the spiritual journey
in the sense that they must not depend on their own efforts
to improve their behavior but establish a deep relationship
with God. When they don't succeed in their efforts, they
also feel powerless. That leads to discouragement unless at the
same time they're transforming their experience of weakness into motives for putting more and more confidence in
the God on whom they are counting to be rescued from
the whole addictive process. Attachment to those emotional
programs for happiness that I mentioned before are so deeply
imbedded that people don't even realize, until they begin the
spiritual journey in earnest, how much energy they put into
them. What the participants in Alcoholics Anonymous have
put their collective finger on is the radical foundation for a
genuine and holistic relationship with God, and that moves
it through levels of acquaintanceship, friendliness, and friendship, to divine union.

TS: Bill's friend, Father Ed Dowling, once wrote an article
about the underprivileged non-alcoholic: people who are
unaware of the Twelve Steps. But help arrived for some of
them because Bill later wrote that many people (non-alcoholics) report as a result of the practice of AA's Twelve Steps
that they have been able to meet other difficulties in life.
Father Thomas, I think most therapists would agree that the

vast majority of non-alcoholics are not aware of their hidden addictions or are in denial of the effect that these are having on their lives. Can you give us a few examples of the more subtle kinds of addiction and how they keep us from realizing a deeper relationship with God?

TK: I like this question. There is a blessing involved in having an obvious addiction that leads to such sad consequences as going to prison, running a car into a tree, beating up one's children, becoming unbearable to live with, losing one's business—the whole string of disasters that people blissfully get into for the sake of a few drinks or a little binge that takes them away from the pain of their own sense of inadequacy. Alcohol isn't the only addiction, of course. There's emotional addiction, sexual misbehavior, overeating, and gambling, to mention just a few. I suppose shopping as a favorite pastime on Saturday afternoons can be an addiction. What is pitiful is that the enormous capacities of human nature for growth, love, freedom, peace, service of others, and reaching out to those in need—all of this immense potential—is simply shoved out of sight in order to find a few moments of satisfaction through over-indulgence in one of those addictions I just mentioned. The awareness that this is not the right way to proceed is present in some degree, but it has no effect on one's conduct; it simply increases the feeling of guilt. Guilt is such a painful emotion that it increases the need to forget it through the exercise of the addiction. The advantage of addiction from the point of view of the addict is that it provides an opportunity to be so preoccupied about planning its expression, thinking about it, reviewing the consequences, and all the rest, that he or she doesn't have time to think of how much pain they have. Discouragement and humiliation, as natural consequences of addiction, can increase the need or craving to get away from the pain. An addiction provides a way of forgetting the kind of pain that can be intolerable in some people.

Bill W. seems to be saying that people who are not involved in an obvious addiction don't realize that much of their behavior is compulsive, or the result of over-identification with cultural norms or symbols of one or other of the instinctual needs. Such people are blissfully unaware of how powerless they are because they can usually fulfill the basic obligations of life. The idea that their motivation is self-centered and selfish doesn't occur to them until they take up a transformative practice like the spiritual journey or the Twelve Steps, or a life that is deliberately aimed at the transformation of our subhuman instincts into the human way of doing things.

Do you want to pursue further that aspect of your question?

TS: I think you answered it pretty well. Addicts with hidden addictions probably need to hit a bottom of some sort, and then we change no matter what the addiction.

TK: Some of our addictions have to do with relating to other people. Some persons are always aggressive, some are always withdrawing, some are not sociable, some tend to be hostile. These ways of relating may depend on one's emotional background that one is not aware of. The insight that psychiatry has contributed to the spiritual journey is that most of our problems are unconscious. We may, for instance, be very generous in offering our services for a party and to bring food, while in actual fact we're more interested in the approval of the guests. Then there are all the subterfuges that people engage in business in order to avoid presenting their product exactly as it is. It doesn't occur to them that there's something inauthentic about this. The real question is, what is your real motive for doing this? Even religious practices can have mixed motivation as is clear in many of the sayings of Jesus that address the human tendency to look for congratulations for our good behavior and generous religious observances such as fasting or giving alms. Obviously these are good deeds and we shouldn't stop doing them, but we shouldn't do them for the motive of obtaining approval and esteem.

TS: Thank you, Father Thomas. This concludes our questions relating to step one.

STEP TWO

*Came to believe that a power greater than
ourselves could restore us to sanity.*

Tom S.: Bill W., in the second step, breaks up newcomers
into five groups. He labels the first group the "belligerent
ones." The next group, "those who have rejected faith." The
next group, "the intellectually self-sufficient man or woman."
The fourth group are those who are "plumb disgusted with
religion." And finally, "the devout." I think the five categories
pretty well summarize the stages of spiritual development
that most sponsors encounter when working with newcomers. There are no boundaries for our discussion today, but I
would like to hear your thoughts regarding the five groups
that Bill Wilson identified.

Thomas Keating: Well, obviously, we have to begin somewhere. Sounds like you have chosen a good approach to
introduce some of these issues. First of all, we need to understand that God is not the same for everybody. Everybody
has his or her own idea of God and his or her own attitude
toward God. Usually, most of us bring with us attitudes and
ideas of God that we received in early childhood. They are
childish and need to mature along with the rest of our human
development. The child thinks of God—if it is given a reli-

gious education of some kind—as a Higher Power whose chief job is to protect it, and to keep it safe and healthy. This is fine. But God has a lot of other aspects that are equally important. As our human maturity continues, we begin to think of God as a just God who rewards good and punishes evil. Most religions suggest that if you follow their precepts, which in general are pretty much the same, God will take care of you. There is often the further idea that you will be prosperous and successful and have a long life with all kinds of blessings.

This idea of God is a little naive. lt is usually battered by life's experiences. For example, we may pray to God as we know Him and there is no answer; or things get worse, or we get worse, as the case may be. To put it in AA terms, our Higher Power transcends anything that we can think about it from the limited perspectives that we have experienced so far in life. That is why meditation is so important. If I asked you who is God, you would normally respond out of your cultural conditioning and religious background, or your irreligious background in the case of people who never got any religious education. Some are overexposed to religious education and practices and may rebel against them. Some are enraged by the misconduct of certain representatives of a particular religion who harm them or harm people they love. Or they just don't like the precepts and the authoritarian demands of this or that aspect of their religion.

So to establish a good attitude with one's Higher Power will take time for such people. In the first four categories you mentioned, it may take a long time. But sponsees can be encouraged to remember that all that AA requires is that they commit themselves to a power higher than themselves. That is to say, they ask the question "Who is God?" with an open mind, as you suggested in your preliminary remarks, and do not try to answer it too fast, because whatever they say in the beginning is not the God who actually is. It is simply a child-ish God or an adolescent God, or an immature adult God, but not the true God. The great benefit of meditation for this category of people is that it invites them to allow God to introduce Himself, instead of trying to answer the ques-tion of who God is. People can harbor very negative feelings about God. For example, "God does not love me; God is a tyrant demanding instant obedience; God is a policeman always on the watch for my least misstep; or, finally, God is a judge who is always ready to bring down upon me the irre-vocable verdict of guilty." Most people in this category will develop corresponding emotions of fear of God. Since you don't think about God at all in non-conceptual meditation, God has a chance to introduce God as God actually is. And in the silence of meditation, or as the preparation that enables us to relate to the mystery of who God actually is develops, then it gives the negative feelings or negatively charged thoughts about God a chance to calm down and to be moderated by the experience of a certain peace and calm that ordinarily comes from the interior silence of meditation itself.

The God that a person who does not like, the God they know, may turn out to be very nice after all. In AA you have a chance to get acquainted and there is no great rush. You are just open to the possibility that God is not the way you think God is from your particular cultural background or human experience thus far. In actual fact, God is existence, and hence must be present in everything that is. So instead of thinking of God, you can think of God's presence, which is the source of everything that is. It is this presence that supports the whole movement of AA. The small group itself can be understood as the Higher Power. So could nature. So could God's presence in the generous service of others.

Many AA people are sponsors helping others in their effort of recovery. God is present in service. God is present in human love. God is present in conjugal relationships. God is present in the flowers, in the sunsets, and in the fields. God is present in all of nature without calling it God. Being open to the Higher Power actually opens us to the fact that all creation is penetrated by a presence that transcends our sensible faculties and introduces us to a world both of mystery and experience.

TS: Years ago, I went to an AA meeting in North Carolina and a woman leading the meeting said she had six years of sobriety, but she said she was an atheist. After listening to her for a while, I realized that she was using the group as her Higher Power. That is the way she existed.

TK: Yes. She does not have to identify the Higher Power with the God of her childhood. "Who is God?" is a question that should be left as a question because it can continue to change as we change, and as our understanding and experience of the Ultimate Reality or Ultimate Mystery continues to expand. So wherever there is an experience that surpasses our narrow ideas and that brings us peace, encouragement, a genuine sense of compassion, forgiveness, and reconciliation there is an encounter with the Higher Power or God. All of these experiences may be a little too soon for alcoholics of the kind that you first mentioned. What we can say to them is be open to the fact that beyond what you feel, there may be a whole world of reality that is very supportive and encouraging if you just open to it and wait for it to introduce itself as you pursue the Twelve Steps. This is especially true if you can sit still, allow yourself to be in silence with God, and move beyond your thoughts of God to whatever God is, without trying to answer that question in rational terms.

TS: Do you think it might be beneficial for a sponsor to take a sponsee, say, in early recovery and just sit with him or her for five minutes in silence without identifying any Higher Power?

TK: I think that would be a good idea. You might be wise to start with maybe a minute of silence because some people, especially in our Western culture, have never experienced silence at all. Some have earphones on all the time even when they sleep, and the noise goes on all night. They don't know what silence is. It is completely unknown to them. Anything that is unknown for a human being tends to be an object of fear. So to start slowly and build up to five minutes seems to me to be a wise way to start.

TS: One of the greatest discoveries I made when I came into AA was to find out that I had a disease. Many of us, at the beginning, think of it as a moral issue or something of that nature. Just to be told that I have a disease and that, while there is no immediate cure, we are on the road to recovery here in AA, gave me so much hope in the beginning. Father Thomas, would you address the "human condition" concept and perhaps describe for us how this deeper understanding of ourselves could be introduced into the early stages of recovery.

TK: It seems to me that one of the great gifts that AA offers to its people is hope. Without hope, it is very hard to proceed in any direction. Fear or discouragement turns one in on oneself and this is the wrong direction to go for recovery. It is precisely our negative attitudes toward ourselves and painful incidents in childhood that are often the cause of our search for compensatory experiences. Or in some cases, it is a getting away from pain through repression into the unconscious where the negative energy remains as an emotion and secretly influences our desires, relationships, and behavior, leading to defensiveness or projection of our feelings onto others. So this issue of being sick, like all diseases, leaves you with the hope that with the proper treatment you may get well.

Hope is very closely related to openness to the Higher Power, because it is precisely because we depended on ourselves and our emotional programs for happiness that we got sick in the first place. These programs are misguided and are mostly based on the instinctual needs that a young child has for security, approval and affection, and power and control. This is not where happiness is to be found. But when one puts an enormous amount of energy into finding happiness there and it is withheld, then off go the afflictive emotions of grief, anger, fear, discouragement, shame, guilt, and others when our programs are frustrated. Then other complicated emotions like envy, jealousy, vanity, ambition, pride, greed, apathy, and anger take over. All of these painful emotions make us unhappy. As long as we have an enormous emotional investment in one of the emotional programs, then every time one of them or all are frustrated, we recycle the same old feelings of anguish. Then we feel pushed into a position of acting out in order to get away from the pain or at least to relieve it. Acting out only reinforces the whole vicious circle, which constantly causes us to make the same mistakes and to ruin one relationship after another: with God, with ourselves, and with other people.

It might also be helpful for the sponsor to be aware that recovery is not something limited to people with an addiction. This misplaced energy is the heritage that we all carry with us as human beings. It is in our genes, you might say. Theologically, some people call it Original Sin. Scriptural people will simply call it the Fall, referring to Adam and Eve and their losing the experience of what true happiness is, which is intimacy with God. The reassurance of being loved and being close to a Higher Power that is tender, loving, considerate, nurturing, supporting—indeed, supporting our life at every level of our being, body, soul, and spirit, is essential. Everybody has this original disease, the lack of intimacy with God. It is not a sin because it is nobody's fault. It is just the way we come into life and develop our self-identity. The identity we have is based on the misguided emotional programs and the idealized image we have of ourselves, which are constantly being challenged by daily life and leave us struggling constantly with emotional turmoil and grief.

An addictive person, especially one who genetically has an addictive personality or who is an obsessive/compulsive personality, is a sitting duck for some kind of emotional high that will relieve him or her of the pain that flows from the consequences of being set up that way. Having an addictive personality intensified by the problems of relating socially to other youngsters, and then to other teenagers, and other adults with belief systems which say "I'm no good"; or, "I have to get away from this pain"; or, "I have to succeed to be happy"; or, "I have to be rich and successful"; or, "I have to control as many situations and people as possible—and God if I can get away with it" —requires psychological and spiritual guidance.

In our culture, a low self-image is epidemic. Many people grow up without a clear self-identity. They will not grow up by acting out their childish emotional programs. AA is a marvelous program of becoming a full human being without being dominated by an addictive program that is tearing you apart. We don't have to live this way. The sponsor is someone who has been through this process and can show compassion as well as the wisdom that comes from experience, and who can say to a sponsee, "Hang in there! You are just getting started. It was tough for me, too. I have seen many other people that thought they would never get out of this swamp. If we attend the meetings and help each other climb out of that swamp by encouragement and working at this program together for true human maturity, we will begin to experience its fruit. And the energy we used to put into security issues, approval by everyone, or controlling everybody, will be available for growth and health. You may still feel the old cravings, but they no longer have the dominating force that used to drive you to seek relief from the pain of frustrated emotions."

TS: I think this understanding of ourselves could be especially helpful in our deeper absorption of the steps.

TK: The term "human condition" is meant to describe, at least as I see it, a virtually universal experience. Almost everybody, regardless of education, can identify with the description of the three basic instinctual needs and over-identification with our group because they have often experienced them in their own lives. Everybody gets upset about something every now and then. Why are they upset? Most people will say somebody did something mean or unkind to them. Not so. Others may have done something wrong to you, but your reaction is still your responsibility. Our over-identification with our feelings and who we think we are is normally the source of our pain. Once you dis-identify with your feelings, you know that you can change them. You are not your feelings. But you have to stay alert. The advantage of a spiritual program like AA is to keep you alert and quick to spot the symptoms of the disease that you now acknowledge.

If you are upset by anything at all, something is the matter with YOU. No doubt something is the matter with other people, too, but you cannot do anything about them. But we can begin our own healing with the help of the Higher Power. It is very important that this is a step early in the AA program because that is what you really have to keep working at. It is not a question of overcoming all our particular feelings, but of acknowledging and recognizing that we have these feelings without identifying ourselves with them. That is a delicate distinction. We usually over-identify with feelings and then act them out. Or we indulge in the feelings and get into a bad mood. They can be overwhelming until they subside. Or we objectify our feelings because they are so painful and project them onto others. We say, "They made me angry." They did not make you angry. You got angry because of something that happened and you did not have to. It is in the letting go of our feelings, after having fully acknowledged them, that brings calm. Here is where the help of one's sponsor is so important to keep reminding us to face the truth of our feelings without identifying with them, acting them out, or objectifying them and blaming them on other people. These strategies simply postpone facing the true problem. Here is where the Higher Power comes in. Nobody is asking you to be perfect. But the goodness of the universe and one's own basic goodness is always inviting you to become fully human and open to the goodness of creation. It is all out there. This is what we need to emphasize in our practices in daily life: recovery is an ongoing process for everyone, not just alcoholics, or those with a classical addiction of some kind.

There is great wisdom in the steps. If you leave one of them out, you slow the process down. So one needs to keep climbing the steps. Failure, falling down now and then, or the struggle with endless, unwanted thoughts and negative feelings are not disasters. *Every* effort to let go of disturbing feelings is a success. Eventually one realizes that we are free from the domination of an attitude or a particular feeling that used to drive us up the wall or plunge us into hours of moodiness, self-depreciation, self-pity, and harsh judgments about others.

TS: Father Thomas, we have discussed the "belligerent one" that Bill mentioned in step two. The next group is the men or women who had "lost or rejected faith." Sometimes AA comes harder to this group. They tried faith and "found it wanting." Bill Wilson calls them the "bewildered ones." As we look at that group, do you have any thoughts that come to mind?

TK: A distinction might be helpful at this point between faith and belief systems. Faith is a surrender to the Higher

Power before it is broken down into particular belief systems. People with belief systems also have faith, but it is expressed through the particular tenets or cultural backgrounds from which these people interpret their experience of God. Basically, faith is an experience of God that calls for a response of trust and self-surrender. It is not an image or concept of God in whatever form that might take in one's particular religion. Faith is prior to any belief system. That is why people of faith have different names for the Ultimate Reality. In the Native American tradition, it is the Great Spirit, the belief that God penetrates all of nature. Muslims believe in Allah, the monotheistic God; Jews believe in the monotheistic God of the Hebrews called Yahweh. St. John the Evangelist identifies God as the Logos, the Word of God, a concept that comes from Greek philosophy and was taken over by the early Christians to explain their belief system. Faith needs some structure in order to explain it to ourselves or to talk about it to others. The only structure available is the one at hand with words, concepts, and philosophical terms taken from one's own cultural tradition.

In the New Testament faith means surrender to God. Those who say, "I can't believe in this God," usually mean, "I can't accept the particular tenets of the religion of my childhood. They were not something I feel I could identify with." But that does not mean they don't have faith. An atheist is really someone who has another religion. For them God is not God. But since God transcends all concepts anyway, it really does not matter that much whether you think of God as God or God as not God. For faith it does not matter, because even if you have a belief system that calls the Ultimate Reality by some name or label, anything you can say about God is more unlike God than God actually is. To be silent before this great and merciful Higher Power is the most important aspect of any belief system. The various religions of the world are simply trying to communicate the spiritual experience of God's presence, which is love.

Today we are seeing an increasing distinction between religion and spirituality. Religion is supposed to bring one to spirituality; that is to say, to the awareness that, as Jesus put it, "God is a spirit and seeks those who worship Him in spirit and in truth." Not only is this a problem for people in regard to negative experiences of religion, there is also the issue of whether we regard God as having a gender. God has no gender. Gender is necessary for procreation and keeping the species in existence. God is the source of all that is without gender specifics.

God is present in everything that is happening and draws people not only through religion, but through nature, art, spiritual friendship, generous service of others, science and the search for the unknown, especially in such disciplines as physics, astronomy, and biology. Some people have been so turned off by religion that they will never go to God through ritual. That does not mean they are excluded from a healthy dependence on the Higher Power that leads to freedom, since God may be drawing them through another attraction or path. God draws people with the cords of Adam, that is through human love, even through their mistakes and failures to observe the moral law. God is everywhere, in everything, and is especially powerful, according to the teaching of Jesus, where you least expect to find Him, that is, in others. For an atheist, the place to find God is in "NOT God."

TS: I was brought up Catholic, altar boy and so forth. The God I believed in was basically the God of my intellect. I memorized my prayers. I said my prayers. I still became an alcoholic. When I came into AA, I started making what I call the twelve-inch trip from the intellect to the heart. I think this is the transformation that many go through in the early stages of AA. We begin to change from, I guess, an intellectual God at the center of our belief system, to a God of the heart.

TK: That is so important for everyone, not just alcoholics. The intellect is very clever in supporting the false-self system and its programs for happiness, and it is always thinking up bigger and better programs for happiness that just don't work. But it is so brilliant and smart that it can figure out all manner of defenses. So no matter how clear it is to everybody else that they are sick, they easily can rationalize themselves into the healthiest specimen on earth, or "this does not apply to me." These self-justifications probably are not deliberate, but nonetheless are very real ways in which we hide from our pain and our true weaknesses. Until we honestly face them, the Higher Power cannot really do much because of the basic freedom that human beings have been given. That is the nature of our particular species. The Higher Power supports what it has made. So we have to consent to move beyond the intellect, accepting it as a great gift, but also recognizing its limitations. As you said, to open the heart to what you really feel before the intellect gets started rationalizing the feeling out of existence does not stop the pain from continuing to exist; but the intellect can pretend that it isn't there when it is.

For intellectual people with an addiction, there is a special problem. How do you get beyond this intellect that thinks it can cure everything on its own. It cannot. That is, I suppose, why some people have to hit bottom. It is only by being clobbered by circumstances and by their abysmal weakness that they finally get the point. The more intelligent they are, the longer it seems to take. To let go of that way of defending oneself is one of the great benefits of AA. It starts right out and tells you, "We came to believe that our lives were unmanageable." They are. This is not a humiliation because everyone else is in the same boat. It just happens that their situation is more serious because in their case the common addictive process has settled on a particular addiction. The intellect loves to rationalize and to create enormous unconscious defenses. Thus, a whole army of professions—psychiatrists, doctors, nurses, and rehab experts—will never be able to persuade them that they are sick. They have to be so sick that they are finally convinced.

TS: I'm very familiar with that group, Father. So we just covered the intellectually self-sufficient man or woman. And we covered those who have lost or rejected faith. There was another group that Bill Wilson spoke about. That was the "plumb disgusted with religion" crowd. This group, Bill writes, "gloated over the hypocrisy of some believers and belabored the sins of some religious people so they could feel superior to them and avoid looking at their own short-comings." Bill wrote, "when they encountered AA the fallacy of their defiance was revealed." They soon concluded "whatever price in humility we must pay, we will pay." Are there any comments you would like to make on this group?

TK: This is an interesting group. I sympathize with them. We expect so much from religious people because of their status. The human condition of weakness and not knowing what true happiness is or where it is to be found, is especially humiliating when experiencing one's inability to observe the kind of behavior patterns that one wishes to achieve. Moreover, if we see other people who are supposed to be well behaved misbehaving, we get indignant. It may be a projection of our own unwillingness to face that we have the same problem. Why should religious people be better than others if we all have a false self?

It is better to put our minds on improving ourselves and not worrying about other people, however religious they claim to be, or being surprised if they fail. The only people who are well integrated are those who have completed a transformative process like the steps. Religion is a way to that level of healing. All along the way, however, we may regress to lower levels of behavior or to childish ways of responding to reality. Why be surprised by that? The bitter experience of the humiliation of our own efforts and our inability to correct our faults are meant to teach us not to judge others at all; that is to say, to make no moral judgment on the behavior of others, even the people who we should be able to count on for good example. Everyone has clay feet. It does not matter how far up the ladder of supposed holiness they might be, the clay feet that belong to the human condition are still there. We have to depend on God to keep them from cracking or breaking in pieces.

TS: The last category is the devout. This is the guy Bill Wilson describes as "full of faith, but still reeking from alcohol." Bill writes that "some in this category have superficial faith, or going to the other extreme, had wallowed in emotionalism and mistaken it for true religious feeling. The fact was, we really hadn't cleaned house so that the grace of God could enter and expel our obsession." Do you have any particular comments regarding this last group?

TK: This is an important one for me because I move in circles that are fairly devout: monks, nuns, priests, and dedicated lay persons who are walking steadfastly on the path of some religious practice. What these people have to keep in mind, and which the spiritual journey itself introduces to us if we get into regular daily meditation, is that there are two levels of being devout. Unfortunately, most of us in our early religious education only hear of one, namely, the conscious motivation of behavior. We must not do this; we must do that. As a result, we make some progress in the spiritual life, but it is very modest. The real issue is the unconscious where we may have enormous investments of energy in worldly objectives such as security, affection, esteem and approval, and power and control. Our secret motivation enters into our conscious motivation and is often very apparent to others. Because of our devout aspirations we are not quite ready to acknowledge our own weaknesses and faults, or we think they are due to somebody else's misbehavior and as I said, we engage in projections. For example, "My parents were not religious" . . . "If only we were living in a better community" . . . "If only my life circumstances could change, I would become whole." This is how the process of transformation works.

The path of devotion only takes you so far. It is only successful when you begin to see how, on the unconscious level, you are secretly permeated with worldly motivation. That is why Jesus, especially in the Sermon on the Mount, attacks these self-centered inner motivations head on. He sums up his concern by saying it is out of a person's heart that good things or evil things come. By "heart," he means our innermost being, and that would include what we call today in psychology "the unconscious." One's devotion is often motivated by worldly desires. For instance, one is practicing fasting during Lent. One is maybe going to some kind of ritual every day and reading the scriptures, fasting, and giving alms. This is wonderful. At the same time, one of the motives for doing that may be that one is in a community where fasting and scripture reading is an honor. So while one is carrying out one's spiritual devotions, a little voice deep inside is saying, "You are better than these other guys" . . . "You are fasting more" . . . "Why don't you give up more sleep? You would give a better example." Those in leadership roles are often afflicted with this problem because they are supposed to give good examples all the time. When they make a few blunders or offend a few people, they get criticized or insulted. Then their idealized self-image as a spiritual leader, someone who manifests the divine in a special way, begins to crumble.

The motivation of the unconscious is extremely important for devout people to understand, especially for people who are leaders in religious circles. If they are unwittingly motivated by desires for power, they will tend to dominate their communities. Or if they have a competitive frame of mind, they will be jealous of other ministers or spiritual directors and feel hurt if the people they are sponsoring decide to go to somebody else. They may even feel this as an unbearable insult. Even if they do not get angry about it, they see that they have these feelings. That should convince them their emotional programs are still firmly present in their unconscious. Hence, we need the healing of the divine therapy, which takes place especially in meditation in which by not thinking for a certain daily period of time, we become aware of our deeper motivations. Daily life also shows it to us by the repetition of patterns of upsetting emotions.

There are many ways in which God invites us through events, other people, in what we read, or our own honest self-reflections, to face ourselves. One of the great gifts of AA is that it starts out with total honesty about oneself. This is where the classic spiritual life also begins, not in our accomplishments, virtues, and devotions. These are all ephemeral and superficial. They look like virtues, but when the chips are down, off go the emotional programs in the unconscious. Only the liberation from our unconscious programs for happiness and the energy that we put into them can free us from the kind of frustration that comes from programs that we feel we have to have in order to be happy. Now, you move to a new attitude. As a result, you might say, "It would be nice if I had power . . . if I possessed all these things I desire . . . if everybody loved me." But if they don't, which is the way things actually happen, it does not bother you that much. You begin to have more peace in daily life instead of being constantly upset by frustration or opposition, or just the ordinary unfolding of daily life and interaction with people who have the same problems. Everyone is in recovery from this perspective and will never fully recover in this life, because we can always improve the level of surrender to the Higher Power and the level of letting go of our desires for happiness that do not work.

The experience of most people on the spiritual path is a recycling of our major instinctual programs for happiness in which we let go of them at ever deepening levels of surrender. Now we know that whether we succeed or not, they are of no consequence to us. We are no longer interested in reward. The love of God has taken over our motivation so that we have more and more freedom just to do God's will. And let the chips fall where they may. If they happen to fall on us, there is no big investment in self anymore to shed a tear over the humiliations of that illusory entity. A distinction that might help is to realize that devotion alone is not what the Gospel recommends. It is a good start, but it is not what the Gospel holds out as the goal of the Christian, which is transformation. Transformation of consciousness involves a radical change of attitude. We had given huge value to the childish instinctual needs of early life for security, affection, esteem and approval, and power and control. Now we choose the Gospel values which arise spontaneously from deep within, as we let go of our emotional programs for happiness and reduce the obstacles to God's presence in our innermost being. In meditation we consent to God's presence and action. That action is healing and affirming at the same time.

TS: You remind me as you spoke, of the activities of Sister Ignatia at St. Thomas Hospital in Akron. She worked with Dr. Bob and alcoholics in the early times. She must have been a wonderful lady. As the alcoholics left the detox and went back to their homes, she would be at the door. The last thing she would say to them was, "Keep AA in one hand and God in the other and you will never have to pick up a drink again." Father Thomas, we can probably close at this point. I just want to thank you so much for being a friend of AA all these years. God bless you.

STEP THREE

*Made a decision to turn our will and our lives
over to the care of God as we understood Him.*

Tom S.: Father Thomas, as the newcomer approaches the third step, he now understands the need to develop some personal concept of God. In our step two conference you used the phrase, "Why not let God introduce Himself?" Could we have your further comments on that phrase to start us today?

Thomas Keating: Your own experience of how God introduced Himself was through various means, the AA meetings, reading the Big Book, and so on.

I was thinking, however, of something even more intimate and profound that takes place in the eleventh step, or in moments of silence, or when one is reflecting on something that you read in the Big Book or one of the slogans that you mentioned. It somehow resonates inside and you just want to sit with that phrase without thinking about it. You simply allow the meaning to penetrate to a level beyond words. So it is in a method like centering prayer, or whenever one moves to a stage of not thinking of anything, even about God.

People who had a strict upbringing or a fundamentalist kind of religious instruction often have ideas of God that are negative or emotionally charged with fear or distrust. Many of these people have come to feel that the only path to healing for them is to give up religion altogether. Any religious word like "faith" or "God" is a buzzword that sets off negative sensations, or perceptions in their unconscious that have fossilized there from early childhood. Obviously, those attitudes are an obstacle to getting to know God or to accepting a Higher Power. Nobody wants to make friends with someone they are scared as hell about. So not thinking of God during a specific time, like a period of twenty minutes or a half-hour in the silence of centering prayer, enables God to introduce Himself with a certain peace, calm, that everything is okay, and even the feeling of forgiveness or of being surrounded by a mysterious and reassuring presence that has no name and that you do not know how to describe, that arises spontaneously. This is what I mean by letting God introduce Himself. He is not as bad as you were led to believe or expected. He is tender, nurturing, concerned, bending over us, so to speak, with great love.

TS: You mentioned twenty minutes to a half-hour: I guess you would not suggest that for a newcomer searching for some introduction to God.

TK: Some people might be able to move into something like this sooner than others. You said it took a couple of years for this introduction to take root in you. In any case, the Twelve Steps are a very effective, well-thought-out, and very experiential way of allowing God to introduce Himself either gradually or more rapidly, depending on temperamental factors or past history. The Holy Spirit can attract people to this kind of relationship quite soon in their conversion. By conversion I mean the decision to start recovery whatever one's difficulties might be.

Whether you are recovering from alcohol or just from the human condition, everybody is called to recovery from something. Sometimes it is just plain childhood. No matter how wonderful our parents, there is always a problem of the child's perception of being left out, or not getting enough credit, or not being loved enough, or not enough attention. This creates needs for compensation and that is something that begins the addictive process.

TS: I think there is a relationship between the depth of the fearlessness required in the fourth step and the depth of our decision in the third step to turn our will and our lives over to God as we understand Him. We do not want our sponsees to spend the rest of their lives on the third step because it only asks for a "decision." But Bill writes "the effectiveness of the whole AA program will rest upon how well and how earnestly we have tried to come to a decision to turn our will and our lives over to the care of God." He also wrote "the AA program can be practiced with success only when step three is given a determined and persistent trial."

Father Thomas, assuming you had the role of a sponsor,

what suggestions would you use to help a sponsee make the third-step decision in depth?

TK: I'm not a sponsor, so I'm not really qualified to respond to your question. I have been a spiritual guide or director of people who have other problems. Basically the challenge is always the same, the courage to turn our lives over completely to God. This is not an issue just for folks in AA. This is everybody's issue if they want to achieve human health, which, as St. John of the Cross says, consists in having a continuous conscious relationship with God.

Just to relate a moment to what I said earlier, if you had a fairly rigid upbringing, or if you just were never interested in God, or if you thought of God simply as the things you hear about on television, you and a lot of us would think of God initially as someone who is only interested in commandments. We may identify God's will with certain behaviors that we are not entirely happy with. We would just as soon not do these things even if it is God's will. So there is a problem that arises from a negative idea of God.

The issue is negative thoughts, at least to us, about keeping all of the commandments, all ten of them. Then usually people throw in a few others that they have picked up from their family or culture, a pile of do's and some dont's. So God is a do-it or don't-er. This kind of image is not appealing to human nature. This step, therefore, has to be delicately inserted between the cracks of those negative values or ideas that were imposed upon us. God has no chance to show that His will can make you happy; reduce the grief and constant emotional upheavals of daily life, and the energy that we put into symbols in the culture stemming from our desires for security, power, control, and esteem and affection.

As children, we do not know how to moderate our desires, and translate the pleasure of instant gratification as happiness. And so, we are bounced around by life's events or circumstances. As a result, we seek various compensations, or we run away from our unfulfilled needs by means of workaholism, distractions of all kinds, and various other ways of trying to bolster our fragile egos.

God has to be allowed to move in and reduce the intensity of the drives for happiness through the gratification of instinctual needs. Like going to a psychiatrist, you have a rapport with God as your primary psychotherapist. The dynamic called transference needs to take place in which you develop trust in your therapist as an authority figure, so that the difficulties you may have had with a father, mother, or teacher are healed through the experience of acceptance by a skilled therapist.

TS: I have to underline what you just said because I had experienced a punishing God in my childhood and I didn't want to turn my will and my life over to a punishing God.

TK: Nobody does.

TS: When I realized and felt internally that I was dealing with a loving God, it was so easy to turn my will and my life over at the depth that is required.

TK: People often need help to change their attitudes to God. The idea of a punishing God, because it comes from earliest childhood, is very deeply embedded in the psyche. Some parents or teachers use God as a kind of sanction or as a weapon to make children behave.

The true God is ready to forgive and, in fact, according to the Gospel, is especially concerned for those whose need is greatest. That is why in the Gospels, Jesus ate and drank with public sinners, manifesting the divine concern for our weakness and the damage that others have done to us knowingly or unknowingly in early childhood, or later, what we may have done to ourselves.

TS: Thanks for those comments, Father. It ties in well with what Bill Wilson wrote: "God is the source of all happiness." We sought it in so many other places.

One final question: for many years I felt a separation from God. He was in His Kingdom and I was here on earth. Would you comment on this misconception?

TK: The Kingdom of Heaven obviously is not an institution or a political program. It's a state of consciousness, and it's specifically the participation in the consciousness that Jesus had of the Ultimate Reality, whom we call God in the Judeo-Christian tradition. The Kingdom of God is

the communication of Christ's own consciousness, coming from His innermost bosom, so to speak. Our problem
is that we have no concept in our ordinary psychological
awareness of the enormous gift that God is offering. One of
the ways that we become aware of this gift is through some
terrible tragedy, a natural disaster or some personal addiction that convinces us of what the first step of AA describes
as the unmanageable character of our lives. . . . And from
that point, one turns oneself over completely to the Higher
Power, as one understands Him; or in the context of the
Kingdom, one turns oneself over completely to this process
of being transformed inwardly and with all our faculties
into the consciousness that Jesus had of the Ultimate Reality, as *Abba*. This God as revealed by Jesus is forgiving, gentle, nurturing, caring, motherly, always leaning over us to
protect us, and secretly accompanying us in our daily lives.
This companionship is available to everybody the moment
they turn to God.

TS: It would seem to me that for the alcoholic this is a great
sign of hope It tells us that good can come out of the bad.
Out of all this pain that we have, good can come out of it.
God loves us just as we are.

TK: Not only that, He loves us in the degree in which we
have need, so that the greater the need, the greater the des-
titution of whatever kind, inwardly or outwardly, the more
we appeal to the infinite mercy of God. Instead of griev-

ing unduly over our wounds, we would be wiser to realize that our desperate need is the greatest claim we have on the infinite goodness and tenderness of God. Pride doesn't want to feel that dependent. It's bad enough to acknowledge our faults. To be totally dependent on God's presence and goodness takes a little while to get used to.

TS: Thank you, Father.

STEP FOUR

Made a searching and fearless moral inventory of ourselves.

Tom S.: Before starting the fourth step, I usually suggest to my sponsees that they write a prayer on the first page of their inventory. If you were asked to compose such a prayer, what words come to mind, Father?

Thomas Keating: I think this would vary with different persons and with personal life histories, temperament, and predispositions. A prayer that would be universal would need to include a prayer for the Holy Spirit's assistance to remember incidents without activating defensive mechanisms. In other words, to be totally open with God, putting down exactly what happened without any commentary, without any defense, and without any exaggeration. Just the facts. God is interested in whether we can accept whatever happened to us or whatever we did to ourselves, just as it is. This is the first step toward true humility, which is the acceptance of the truth about ourselves.

TS: That sounds just like a prayer, just the way you said it. In step four, Bill Wilson described a universally recognized list of major human failings as the seven deadly sins of pride, greed, lust, anger, gluttony, envy, and sloth. He wrote that pride often justifies our instinctual excesses for sex, security, and power. Pride seems to be such an immeasurable evil. Would you comment on pride, and how it works to justify these excesses?

TK: Pride is extremely subtle and well-equipped to defend itself even from the obvious truth. We have only to consult our own experiences to see how often we have deceived ourselves in practical life situations. Pride usually presupposes ourselves as the center of the universe. This is not the case. Pride is usually defined as the excessive love of our own excellence. There are things about us that are wonderful, such as our basic core of goodness, which is inalienable. We are made in the image of God, a participation in God's own life. Pride attributes to oneself the gifts of God. We are inclined to take pleasure in our natural talents as if we owned them and were responsible for them. Our very being is God's gift to us. Since God is truth, He expects us to recognize that this is a gift and not an inalienable right. We are creatures in the sense that we did not make ourselves. Pride even gets into our spiritual journey, and we may attribute to ourselves our good behavior and our virtues. We have to undo these ideas. Effort in the spiritual journey is chiefly about finding out that it doesn't work. The harder one tries, the worse one gets, unless one turns one's activity over completely to God and follows God's inspiration. God doesn't take away our faults right away, because if He did, we would be likely to attribute

it to our own efforts. It's a painful process for Him as well as
for us to have to put up with our misdeeds. They are not as
bad as pride, however, which is attributing our good deeds
to ourselves and which is not only ridiculous, but insulting
to God and to the truth of God's gifts. At the same time, the
humble acceptance of who we are is only half the story, and
if we get to the first step, it has to be complemented by the
third step in which we turn our lives over completely to God
and to God's will. Without that balancing disposition, the fact
that our life is unmanageable may cause us to give up the
work of recovery in total despair, after a number of fruitless
efforts to improve.

TS: Yes, many of us in AA often go back to the third step.
There's a little rejuvenation here because turning our lives
over to the care of God is the basis for the rest of the steps.

TK: Yes, it is crucial.

TS: I have another question. Bill Wilson wrote that the newcomer first looks at those personality flaws that are acutely
troublesome and fairly obvious. He makes a rough survey of
his conduct concerning his primary instincts for sex, security,
and society. Bill also wrote that there is a great need for a
cross examination of ourselves, ruthlessly, and to determine
what personality traits demolished our security. He was also
familiar with the writings of Karen Horney, a noted psycho-
analyst of her day for whom he had a great respect. He once
mentioned that Miss Horney's writings regarding the taking

of a moral inventory were the best he had ever seen. Would you comment, or perhaps capsulize for us, Miss Horney's suggestions?

TK: It's forty or fifty years ago that I read her book *Neurosis and Human Growth*. There she shows how the pride system, as she calls it, develops from the early beginnings of life and the difficulties of childhood, and how the idealized self-image develops, in which we have a firm conviction that we are or have to become a certain set of virtues or accomplishments in order to be who we think we are or should be. As I remember it, she shows, with enormous skill, how this process develops. The process could also be called the development of the false self or the homemade self— the self that develops as the survival mechanism in early childhood to deal with the frustration of the instinctual needs that the child feels are not being provided. Frustration inevitably confronts the instinctual needs of the child for security and survival, approval, affection and esteem, and power and control. She develops masterfully how the result of identifying happiness as the gratification of those instinctual needs forces the psyche to extraordinary lengths to protect its idealized self-image, which is basically rooted in pride.

TS: In writing about the natural instincts for power, security and companionship, Bill Wilson wrote that they "often far exceed their proper functions and even tyrannize us." He said we need to ask how, when, and where did our natural desires warp us. He also wrote that "alcoholics should see that instincts running wild in themselves are the underlying cause of their destructive drinking, and instincts on the rampage balk at investigation." Father Thomas, it seems that Bill is herein describing the characteristics of what we spoke about, which you described as self-development in our own likeness, rather than in the likeness of God. The false self also balks at investigation. From your perspective, what can a fourth-stepper do to make his effort "searching and fearless" and get past this balking stage? Do you have any suggestions?

TK: I couldn't agree more with Bill Wilson's evaluation of how deeply entrenched activity rooted in instinctual needs, and their gratification, actually is. It seems to me that for the inventory you are starting with people who cannot possibly reach that degree of honesty at the first shot. So, if they can write down what actually happened and they can freely acknowledge the source of activity that led to their addiction, and to real problems of conscience for them, that would be a good start. I presume that in the course of the Twelve Step program one returns again and again to one's inventory. But a good sponsor who has been over this road and has suffered some of the same problems would be able to point out, on the basis of what this person reveals, certain lines for further pursuit. He might say, "You said this. . . . Have you thought of where this fault might have come from? Under what circumstances did this activity proceed?" And then, "Why did it happen? Is there a pattern of activity here, based on some kind of frustration of your basic instinctual needs for security, power, or approval?"

Thus, the sponsor would invite the person who is making the self-inventory to deepen his or her insight. If they continue to work together, it will open up. If they also have a relationship with the Higher Power, they will be aware that this Higher Power is also working. In the Christian tradition we call this the Holy Spirit. Once they have acknowledged the unmanageability of their lives and turned them over to God, they would be engaging in what might be called the divine psychotherapy, in which the light of the Holy Spirit would accompany their inventory and deepen their insight into the causes of the negative circumstances described there. The divine light would also invite them, with great gentleness and firmness, to look into the causes of what they now see to have been the source of their present problems.

TS: It's amazing to see how much Bill Wilson's writings and your thoughts coincide.

TK: We're trying to talk about the same thing. The spiritual journey is going in the same direction as AA and involves the same essential steps.

TS: Is it just a different wording? Forty years later, we know things that we didn't know then.

TK: That's true. There's a lot more psychological know-how available that I'm sure Bill W. would have used.

TS: He once described one type of alcoholic, doing the fourth step, as the "depressive type," who is apt to be swamped with guilt and self-loathing, the very process that led him to the bottle. I find it useful in these cases to point out to the sponsee that he is a good person at his center. My sponsor used to say that "God doesn't make junk." The sponsor often comforts such persons by sharing his own faults and defects, past and present. As you listen to this, is there any special spiritual practice, prayer, or reading that comes to mind that might be helpful to such depressive types?

TK: Yes, self-loathing and its consequent depression, discouragement, lack of self-esteem, and hopelessness are very serious problems. These need to be opposed vigorously by the sponsor. It seems to me that much depends on the background of the sponsee. Usually those who are most sensitive to their faults are religious people who also have a heritage of right and wrong that often involves heavy guilt feelings for their misdemeanors. Unfortunately, this can be reinforced by certain passages in the Gospel and the Hebrew bible. It would be helpful for the sponsor, working with people with a religious background, especially a Judeo-Christian background, to arm themselves with texts that emphasize the boundless mercy of God, such as the parable of the Prodigal Son. This passage has been a great source of consolation to many people with difficulties like this.

But you already hit on the most essential thing to keep reminding them, which is to affirm their basic goodness. In biblical language, this means we are made in the image of God. This image can never be erased by any activity whatsoever. God's presence and light within us supports us every nanosecond of time. All of human misery is simply layers of junk that covers this and so it's sometimes easy to identify the junk as ourselves, instead of recognizing that junk is our enemy disguised as misguided or distorted activity, not our true self that remains a brilliant jewel even though it's at the bottom of a pile of garbage. These people need to be encouraged to start shoveling with the firm confidence that if they get to the bottom of the pile of this junk, they will find their own immeasurable beauty: God's gift that can never be destroyed by any misconduct whatsoever.

TS: I often remind newcomers that they are good persons at the center. No one tells them that when they are reaching the bottom of their destructive drinking . . . it's just the opposite.

TK: Yes, it's so important that the sponsor keeps returning to the fundamental truth of our basic goodness as human beings. These people can never hear it enough. And in this culture, even without an addiction, there are many youngsters who are brought up in an atmosphere of quasi-rejection or indifference. They may be orphans, feel rejected by peer groups, or because of temperament or childhood may never succeed in a highly competitive society. All those things reinforce the destructive idea that "I'm no good, that nobody loves me"; or, "I'm unlovable." They never heard that they have a basic core of goodness that makes them precious to God no matter what happens. God always works to heal the emotional wounds of a lifetime, beginning with the damage that we suffered from others in early childhood when we were too weak to defend ourselves or to evaluate the negative feelings that we may have suffered. Many children have been subjected to abuse of one kind or another.

TS: The sponsors themselves have to remember to continuously get their own spiritual nourishment, then we can pass it on. We can't give what we don't have. So we have to go to the spiritual well ourselves through whatever practice we have adopted.

TK: It's presumption for anyone to teach or counsel someone in the spiritual journey or in a self-help program who isn't doing it. As soon as you stop doing it, you should resign as a teacher or sponsor. You've lost contact with a fundamental dynamic of holistic health and hence with the goal of every therapy, spiritual direction, or sponsorship.

TS: There is one remaining item. Bill wrote once of the idea of someday extending the moral inventory of AA to a deeper level and making it an inventory of psychic damages. In 1956, he wrote about reliving actual episodes of inferiority, shame, guilt, and anger, truly reliving them in our minds and thereby reducing them. This ties in a little with Karen Horney and her writings. I wonder, instead of intentionally reliving them in our minds, wouldn't it be better to just turn them over to God's care through centering prayer or other practices?

TK: It sounds like you are talking about Gestalt therapy. This is a specific kind of therapy in which you re-enact relationships that were painful. The purpose is to repeat the actual event in a dramatic way to stir up the same feelings that you experienced when it happened, so that you can deal with it, or handle it differently. This is a good practice. It's not contradictory to other kinds of spiritual help that we might be getting. It would be up to the sponsor and the sponsee to decide whether they want to do this. No therapy works unless you cooperate. You have to be willing and choose it yourself.

In some cases, just doing a spiritual practice would produce the same effects. It's like saying that you expect God to do everything. Yes, He does everything. But He makes use of secondary causes such as medical advice and therapies, and we shouldn't rule out other means that could reinforce the process of transformation that is the specific work of the spiritual journey and contemplative prayer.

TS: Thank you for your viewpoint on that. We are at a point here where we can move on to the fifth step, unless you have some remaining comments on the fourth step.

TK: I am ready to move on.

STEP FIVE

*Admitted to God, to ourselves, and to another
human being the exact nature of our wrongs.*

Tom S.: Many AA's at first try to delay step five. Some
have an intense fear and reluctance to do it. Certain dis-
tressing or humiliating memories, we tell ourselves, ought
never to be shared with anyone. Bill Wilson wrote that
"without a fearless admission of our defects to another
human being, we could not stay sober." So, Father Thomas,
what thoughts or comments come to mind at this juncture
regarding step five?

Thomas Keating: This step is a very profound and realistic
insight into the spiritual journey and the process of holistic
health, if you prefer to use language other than spiritual. In
the Christian ascetical tradition, the revelation of one's faults
and the discovery of one's interior motivation down to the
very roots are always recommended as an essential part of the
first years of one's spiritual journey. It is only gradually that
many people acknowledge the full extent of their faults or
see the mixed motivation contained in their good deeds. The
early Irish monks were famous for reporting their faults every
day to their spiritual guides. These were not necessarily serious faults, but the kind of faults that Bill W. referred to as the

basic causes of all addictions: what he called the seven deadly sins, sometimes called the capital sins in Christian moral theology. They are essentially scenarios based on the ongoing frustration of our instinctual needs that are likely to translate into harmful activity, such as trampling on the rights and needs of others and our own true good in order to get what we want or to get away from what we don't want. The capital sins are not sins but tendencies to actual sin. With the help of a sponsor, we can gradually realize that underneath our sinful activity, like rotten fruit on a tree, are the roots of the tree out of which this negativity is emerging. Until we eliminate the disease in the roots of the tree, there will always be fruits that are less than good. Good fruit can only come from a tree with sound roots. This step is crucial to establishing the fruit of the first step, which is the conviction that our life is unmanageable. The next question is why is it unmanageable? The inventory and the sixth step begin to explore that in depth. That exploration makes the first step really work, and leads to the turning over of ourselves and our will into the hands of the Higher Power. The more we see the roots of the problem, the more we realize that we can't handle it by ourselves. Hence, we turn ourselves over to the divine therapy and allow God to do what is necessary. AA could be looked upon as a self-help program, only it's much more than a self-help program. It's a spiritual program in which the healing is primarily coming from God, and we submit.

TS: There is a little saying in AA: "If you don't do the fifth step, you're going to pick up a fifth." Many people have a hard time with the fifth step in AA, because we have to talk to somebody outside of ourselves and reveal this stuff from the past.

TK: The Fathers and Mothers of the Desert used to make a great deal of this process. They used to say that when you reveal your temptations like the capital sins, you get a whole new insight into their power over you. It is by externalizing them that you see them. Some spiritual writers have said that that is all that's required to heal many temptations— share it with one's spiritual guide or sponsor. As soon as you hear yourself saying the truth, you're in a whole new world. Temptation looks so good when you keep it to yourself. By hiding the temptation through whatever motive—it's usually pride—you only make it worse. But as soon as you expose it to the outside air, you get a clearer view and you see it as the temptation that it is. You also expose it to the objective judgment of another person who loves you and is ministering to your needs. You are more likely to come up with an objective plan about how to deal with this stuff. In the monastery, we make a big point of being totally open with our spiritual director. Confession is about deliberate sins. Spiritual direction is about the root or causes of our sins. Hence it needs to be done much more frequently, especially in the first years of one's conversion. The false self, or pride, is so subtle that unless you are completely open and frank about everything, you cannot gain freedom from these secret movements of pride that say: "Oh well, it's not important that I say anything about this." Whatever you know you don't want to say is the thing you should say first—get the biggest thing off your mind! If you have ever heard confessions, you know that most people tend to leave the worst stuff to the end. That's how you know what penitents most want to hide. Encourage them to say first whatever they would rather not say at all. Then it's done. An enormous inner freedom comes from the ability to deal with whatever thoughts go through your head. Thoughts are not the problem; it's what you do with them. Hiding them is the worst thing you can do.

TS: One of the things that I found most helpful in the fifth step when a sponsee is having a problem with it, is to send him back to the third step, because if we really feel that we've turned our will and our lives over to the care of God, what do we have to worry about?

TK: A good point. That would be a great form of spiritual guidance.

TS: I have to admit that when I went to confession, I was a great mumbler, but I'll tell you something else. After the fifth step, when I went to confession, I had the grace to go and just sit across the table from the priest, and it was no longer the thought of "confessional," but of joining the human race. You said "freedom," and that's what it was, it was freedom.

TK: The perfection of this step is the willingness to tell God and anybody in the world what you've done. By being willing to be completely vulnerable to everybody's judgment of you, you are completely free of any form of pride. There is a certain prudence, of course, in limiting this to one person, because the whole world doesn't need to know all the details. The willingness to tell anybody is manifested in telling it to the particular sponsor whom you have chosen. That is hard enough. It will result in inner freedom—"What difference will it make if everybody knows what I am?" . . . At the end of life there may be a re-run of your whole life for the benefit of anybody in the next world who is interested. You might as well get used to the fact that everybody will know exactly who you are and what you've done. The willingness to be totally truthful is the triumph over pride and the greatest safeguard not to be caught by the subtleties of the temptations that arise from pride.

TS: One final question, Father. Bill Wilson wrote that our first practical move toward humility must consist of recognizing our deficiencies. While step four was a humiliating experience, it didn't mean that we had yet acquired much humility. Bill Wilson begins discussing humility in step five when he says that "it puts us on the right road to genuine humility." Humility is also an underlying theme in future steps. Father Thomas, will you give us your thoughts on humility, how it eludes us, and how important it is in our lives?

TK: This is a great subject because it is the most fundamental religious disposition. It undergirds all of the stages of

the spiritual journey. It gets deeper as we go along. Humiliation is the way to humility. So you have to go through
the fifth step. It can be tortuous for some people to have to
admit what they are doing in secret, or what their foolish
thoughts are, and all that stuff. But you gradually get used to
it. You lose the sense of shame and you gain more and more
inner freedom. The point may come when you actually love
your weaknesses and faults, because they keep you humble.
The feelings of shame and humiliation give way to a loving
acceptance of the truth and a complete trust in God's infinite
mercy. To have our faults made public is sometimes one of
the greatest gifts of God. It is one thing to fall on your face
in private, and another thing to do so for the benefit of the
media. You can be crucified by other people's knowledge of
your faults. This happens in the press all the time. Humility is
to be content to be poor and weak and to accept the proof of
it in one's life, instead of wishing that they hadn't happened.
In other words, now we take a certain satisfaction in having
proved that we are totally dependent on God, not because we
want it to hurt other people, if that was what it was about, but
simply the fact that now we have no pretensions. We're not
asking anybody to think that we are good, because we now
see that whatever good we have comes from God. We don't
deny that we have this basic goodness, but we acknowledge
that we have made a mess of our lives—they are unmanageable—and that God is healing us. Instead of grieving because
of our sins, we realize that God has used them for our great
benefit.

There is no vindictive attitude in God. God is not a punishing God. Whatever suffering happens to us is part of the healing and transformation process. As soon as we turn our wills over to God, everything we have ever done that was harmful or wrong is totally forgiven. We still have to deal at times with the consequences in our lives or our misdeeds like an addiction, but we know that God loves us, and that no matter what we do God will continue to love us. We can count on God to keep us moving toward the transformation that is the goal of creation. Our faults are a constant motive for turning our self over completely to the Higher Power. St. Thérèse of Lisieux wrote, "I feel joy not only when I recognize that I'm imperfect and weak, but above all when I feel that I am." In other words, she enjoyed feeling the weakness of human nature in order to glorify God's work in her. And she adds, "If God could find a soul weaker than I, He would fill that soul with even greater graces than I have received." She is now not only a saint, but a Doctor of the Church, an approved teacher whose doctrine is officially certified as one of the greatest in the history of the Christian religion.

TS: Thank you for that insight. Do you have further thoughts on that humility topic that we might not have covered?

TK: In view of our discussion, some of the classical definitions of humility might be enlightening. For example, humility is the truth. That is to say, humility is the capacity to accept whatever happens, peacefully. Then you can decide whether God is calling you simply to accept the situation, or to do something to improve or correct it. Humility is a constant and permanent disposition that puts one in tune with the universe and with whatever is happening in the present moment, whether to oneself or others. It opens one to a broader view of the human condition, so that we don't see tragedy as just tragedy, or disaster as just disaster, or our weakness as just weakness. Rather, we see them as a real part of reality, but still not nearly as important as the truth of God's infinite mercy and the fact that God's justice in this world is totally at the service of His mercy. Humility is very close to trust, or the virtue of hope in the Christian tradition. You might say that the whole journey might be summed up as humble hope. Hope here is not the emotion of hope, the expectation that things will get better, or the desire for certain goals that are possible but hard to attain. The theological virtue of hope is based not on what we've done, whether good or bad, but simply on the fact that God is infinitely powerful and infinitely merciful, right now. So, it thinks neither of the past or of the future; it thinks nothing of reward; it simply is in the present moment, totally dependent on God's mercy, and confident that that mercy is boundless. If you're convinced that you have the infinite mercy of God, what more do you need? You have everything. Everything is contained in that hope. Thérèse says that "we can never have too much confidence in God who is so powerful and so merciful." And she writes, "If I had on my conscience every conceivable crime, I would lose nothing of my confidence, but with my heart breaking with love, I would throw myself into the arms of God, and I am certain that I would be well received."

In this view of humility, our weakness becomes the motive for boundless confidence in giving ourselves over to God. It's the fulfillment of all the other steps of AA. We know that whatever happens, the love of God is always with us and that He will turn even our failures into perfect love.

TS: Your insight on humility, it is hoped, will help many in AA and outside AA.

TK: It's the teaching of the Christian mystics. Humility is the basic disposition of all true religion.

STEP SIX AND STEP SEVEN

Tom S.: In our past meetings, we discussed steps two through five in depth, and touched on some special subjects concerning Bill Wilson and the topic of emotional sobriety.

In AA, we submit to steps six and seven without any reservation whatsoever and we move forward in our sobriety; but there is one nagging question that remains unanswered. And that is, why after taking steps six and seven, do the very same character defects continue to arise in our lives, sometimes intensely? Father Thomas, would you explain why the human condition is a major part of the answer to this nagging question?

Thomas Keating: This question calls for a bit of psychological reflection and knowledge of the way a human being develops after it comes into the world. The emotional life really begins in the womb. How fragile the human person is in its developmental stages, especially in the first four years of life, is pretty well-known by psychology today, and it needs to be addressed if we hope to provide an adequate response to this question.

TS: Just to interject a moment. Some years ago we were studying Sigmund Freud and the discovery of the unconscious at the turn of the last century. Bill Wilson was aware of that development and also corresponded with Carl Jung regarding psychological matters.

TK: There has been a great deal of development in psychological thinking and experience since then. The fundamental insight of Freud is of extreme importance for self-knowledge of any significant kind and also for the development of the spiritual life, because it means that not only do we have to deal with our conscious life, but with the dynamics that are present in the unconscious, which are secretly influencing our conduct and our decisions all our life long, unless we are involved in deep psychoanalysis or psychotherapy, or unless we begin the spiritual journey as understood in its classical form. It is a process that gradually releases repressed material in the unconscious and the compensatory means we might have taken to hide the pain of traumatic experiences.

The question is, what are we so traumatized about? The primary answer to this is that we are made for happiness and when we enter the world, we have no criteria as to what that is. The infant is totally immersed in its experience of the senses and identified with its mother in the first year-and-a-half. So it has little or no self-consciousness. As it begins to objectify the external world, it develops a subject who is doing this objecti-fication. This is the birth of self-consciousness. It grows with-out a practical experience of what true happiness is. Thus, it has no experience of a loving God.

The various religions of the world have tried to explain this phenomenon in various ways. In some Christian tradi-tions, it became known as Original Sin or in a more general sense, the fall of Adam and Eve through disobedience to God and the loss of the delightful interaction that, according to the book of Genesis, took place between God and our first parents. The details of that story tell us that there is some-thing seriously missing in our consciousness.

To put it more exactly, the fact that something is miss-ing in our consciousness needs to be explained as we grow up and gradually reach the age of reason. We ask questions: Why do I feel this way? . . . What is happiness? . . . What is the meaning of life? . . . And although these questions are buried under the concerns of everyday life, there are certain periods of our growth when they become urgent, such as in the mid-teens. There's a point at which the brain is fully developed and its intuitive aspects are in place and ready to function. Although in the late teens the need to ask ques-tions about the meaning of life arises, they are pushed onto the back burner in our culture. The urgency of academic demands made on young people, in order to prepare to earn a living, predominates over all other considerations. In addition, there is the need to develop relationships and a social life, which are normally very significant for teenagers. Thus, they don't have time to address the questions that are emerging from the deeper levels of their being. Moreover, they don't have training as to how to do this, and none of their friends is quite ready to talk about it either. Thus, other interests overshadow this fundamental one. In any case, we come to full self-reflective self-consciousness around the age of thirteen or fourteen, without the experience of what true happiness is. To state the issue in another way, without the experience of God, who is happiness, we have a desperate need for happiness, but only the vaguest idea of where it might be found. And so we start experimenting with little guidance or criteria of an either interior or social kind.

But, as I say, few people have the time, inspiration, motivation, or guidance to do that early in life. So what happens in the concrete? The three instinctual needs of human nature that we're born with are: security and survival; power or control; and affection, esteem, and approval. These are genuine values and essential to get through the vicissitudes of early life. If we don't have adequate gratification of those needs, the average child will just roll over and die. The problem is that the child interprets the gratification of its instinctual needs as happiness, and hence if these are frustrated—that is, if its security, power, and affection needs are withdrawn—the child experiences its evolving human development as painful or frustrating. The more these needs are withheld, the more intense is this pain and trauma, and some of this painful material is likely to be repressed into the unconscious. This undigested emotional material is ware-housed in the body in the form of afflictive emotions such as grief, shame, humiliation, anger, discouragement, loneli-ness, desolation, and the sense of rejection. These feelings are very serious in an infant; it can't survive in a healthy way with a steady diet of this stuff. From this predicament, the need to repress, especially incidents that were particularly humiliating, such as experiences of abandonment or abuse, is overwhelming. Some parents are not good at showing affection, or they're not around, or the child interprets the disappearance of a parent as rejection. The lack of knowing where true happiness is to be found is called *illusion* in the Christian system and Hindus call it *maya*. In other words, we begin to perceive the world the way we want it to be. In this developing situation, the child's self-consciousness begins to build a kind of homemade self. This is called today the *false self*, which is the self as the center of the universe around which his or her faculties, feelings, desires, and expectations circulate like planets around the sun. Thus, any event or per-son coming into that sphere of influence, or magnetic field of emotional need, is interpreted not on the basis of its own value or its objectivity, but on whether or not it serves the instinctual desires of the child. For example, does it fit into my expectations or desires for satisfaction and the gratifica-tion of my needs for security, affection, and control?

The formation of the individual self is another term for the formation of the false self. This self is called *false* because it is a self that responds not to reality, but to the emotional programs for happiness that the child formulated very early in life. In fact, by four years of age the false self is pretty well in place. It then moves on to look for support systems in the environment. From roughly four to eight years of age the socialization period occurs. This greatly complexifies the emotional programs for happiness, for security, approval, and control. Thus, this poor little creature begins not only to exercise or feel the needs of this, but begins to take possession of this false subjectivity and to impose demands on its peers, parents, teachers, and every- body else. The symbols of security, affection, and control in the culture become desperate needs. All the energies of the child are then put in the service of fulfilling them. Of course, a moderate amount of pleasure through the gratifi- cation of these programs for happiness contains true values. Everybody needs some acceptance, some security, and a lot of love. However, if the child rightly or wrongly perceives these needs as being withheld, then day after day he or she is experiencing conscious or unconscious demands for happiness, pleasure, or gratification in these three ways. The child is in competition with everybody else who has the same exaggerated needs, and hence there are going to be conflicts and explosions, that is to say, events that trigger the frustration of these conscious and unconscious needs, and then, off go the afflictive emotions. That's the spontane- ous nature of the way the emotions work. If our desire for approval is frustrated by criticism, then immediately frustra- tion will manifest in the form of afflictive feelings. If the immediate reaction is anger, that may involve feelings of revenge. Feelings always set off immediate reactions in the body. If it's fear, the fight or flight syndrome goes off, and adrenaline starts filling the blood stream. There's no way to feel at peace again until the liver has filtered out all this adrenaline, and this process may take a few hours. The more intense the emotional frustration, the longer the lingering effects of it will remain in the body, and we will then want to get away from these feelings by some kind of distraction.

So you pick up a phone and call a friend, or you go to the movies, or you turn on the television, or you read a book, or you go to sleep, or you reach for a cup of coffee. You've got to do something to use up that energy in order to find a certain relative peace of mind again. Obviously, if this happens several times a day, you've got a program for human misery. The repeated frustration becomes the center of our attention, and we have to invent ways of avoiding the pain. The most accessible one is to start thinking of something else or to engage in commentaries about the situation that the imagination readily provides and that may actually reinforce the intensity of the afflictive emotion.

If you have anxiety and don't drop it right away, it turns into fear. Fear then leads into panic. If you give in to feelings of irritation, it turns into anger, then into rage, and finally into a form of temporary insanity.

Some crimes are the result of this emotional excess for which a person is not really responsible, but which may do terrible damage to other people. One of the purposes of meditation as a healing practice is to quiet the mind and to cultivate the experience of peace in the psyche, so that the intensity of the emotions of grief and anger are mitigated to some degree.

As a result, if you bring a reduced demand for the emotional programs for happiness to be gratified in daily life, you will begin to feel more at peace and have more energy for things that are really useful, such as the service of God and the needs of others; or if you're on the spiritual journey, for the vigorous pursuit of meditation, prayer, and the service of others.

We're talking now about the most fundamental problem in human beings: the emotional programs for happiness that cannot possibly work in the adult world. Number one, you're in competition with six and a half billion other people trying to do the same stupid thing. People madly seek all kinds of ways to find symbols in the culture that will give them this gratification. Thinking is one of the best ways of hiding the contents of the unconscious. Hence in meditation, one moves off the ordinary level of psychological awareness deliberately in order to cultivate the spiritual level of our being, which is the level of intuition and the spiritual will. As a result, one begins to have space in which to evaluate one's desires and longings and to moderate them, at least insofar as one can.

This brings us to the third consequence of the human condition. I mentioned illusion, not knowing where true happiness is; and concupiscence, which is looking for it in the wrong places—or too much in the right places. The third one is especially devastating, and this is if we ever find out where true happiness is to be found, our will is too weak to do anything about it anyway. This is a rather dim view of human nature, but it happens to be true. Contemporary psychology and various self-help groups have tried to address this problem, too. They have succeeded in providing us with a complete diagnosis, you might say, of what's contained in those three areas of illusion, concupiscence, and weakness of will. You just have to read any book on dysfunctional families, family systems theory, or codependency, to have a clear idea of what the consequences of what scripture calls the Fall really are.

Here is someone coming into adulthood and reaching the natural development of the powers of reasoning that some anthropologists call the *mental egoic level* of consciousness. It arrives at adulthood with all the habits that lead to human misery firmly in place and a body filled with repressed emotional material that has never been processed. We are not aware of the dynamics of the unconscious and sometimes there are serious problems, especially if we experienced years that we interpreted as oppression, rejection, and the withdrawal of the support systems that we needed or had a right to.

TS: In your view, how does the sixth step help to uproot our deeply entrenched character defects?

TK: The sixth step says to our great surprise that we became willing that our faults be cured. This is a far cry from what one would expect.

Now that we have taken the path to human whole-
ness, you'd think we would be exhorted to exercise our will
power to moderate our instinctual needs and to practice service of others and all the other things that lead to the full
development of a human being. Not according to AA. This is
a marvelous insight into the actual situation of human nature.
These programs for happiness are deeply rooted and strong
and perhaps half of them are hidden in the unconscious and
motivated by repressed material that we don't even know
about, let alone think of changing. The exercise of willpower
to correct our faults and failings is a misunderstanding of
how sick we are. That is to say, we can't really do anything to
heal ourselves without the power of God's help.

A mistaken idea of how to relate to God at this point in
our spiritual development often afflicts people on the spiritual
journey who do not have an addiction. They just have a false
self and think that now that they perceive the path to true happiness, all they have to do is decide to do it. So they won't eat
this, and they'll fast, get up earlier than anyone else, be much
more patient with the children, won't criticize others, keep
the Ten Commandments. It doesn't happen. Their best efforts
end up in miserable defeat, and they crawl off to confession or
to some counselor or to someone to encourage them to try
harder. To try harder is rarely good advice. To trust more is good
advice. To entrust ourselves completely to God's mercy is the
most enlightened of all the responses to the human condition.

Our faults are not going to go away by our efforts. But
oddly enough, since it is so easy to get rid of them just by

being willing, according to the text of AA, it implies the possibility that we may love our faults, and that's why they don't go away. God is willing to take them away. We are not willing, even though we may kid ourselves, "All I have to do is to make up my mind to be good and I'll be good." It's not going to happen that way. The first movement toward release from the false self, and the whole complex of emotional programs for happiness, is not going to happen unless we are completely willing. This is what the Gospel means by repent. "Repent" means, "change the direction in which you're looking for happiness." If we are not yet willing to change, then we don't change, even though we may make efforts (or half-hearted efforts) to change our behavior. When the chips are down, or when the temptation is strong, when we need compensation for our wounds, whether emotional, physical, or spiritual, then off go the habitual patterns, and we're flat on our face again with our human miseries.

Perhaps you would like to pursue that aspect of the question further since I spent so much time on the context or background.

TS: It was very necessary, Father. We needed your explanation because so many of us are somewhat frustrated when we get to the sixth and seventh steps. Our willingness is there but we still have our character defects. You've explained why, with the explanation of the conscious and the unconscious, and the false-self system that derails our best efforts.

One of the assets that we've got, in our twelve step

efforts in AA, is the sponsor. The sponsor moves us along. Even though we've done the sixth and seventh imperfectly, he moves us into the eighth step and the ninth step, and although we're doing each one of these imperfectly, he knows that we're moving toward the eleventh step, where we enter the regular practice of prayer and meditation, the antidote, I believe, to the false-self system. So I have to say Bill Wilson certainly was divinely inspired in writing these steps; even their sequence was a key inspiration.

TK: I would like to add one other aspect. Having heard your reflections, I understand the sponsor is really speaking to the conscience of the sponsee to help him or her listen to the reality that the unconscious is trying to express. It's hard to do this alone because nobody is quite that honest. The sponsor is trying to keep you honest and willing to face your faults as they emerge. It took Bill Wilson a little while to realize that beyond the conscious efforts that don't work is the further problem of having repressed material in the unconscious, which prevents us from an honest response. The sponsor is like the Holy Spirit that tries to get us to listen to our motivation, and not to deny it or to project it on others; to feel our feelings just as they are and not to be afraid of them; and to accept the support of another person who has been through this process. The sponsor can say just the right word at the right time. The Holy Spirit is present with the sponsor and the sponsee when they're seriously seeking together to negotiate the sixth and seventh steps. The sponsee thinks, "Oh, I want to get rid of this fault so much." Yes, "so much," but not fully. God waits for us to fully want to let go. That's when you finally start praying that He take your faults away. They will dissolve rather quickly in that atmosphere. The problem is we don't realize how deeply entrenched they are. In other words, the Holy Spirit takes us to the first step. Whether you're in AA or in the spiritual journey, the first step is pretty crucial. People who are leading respectable human lives are somewhat naive about the depth of their capacity for wrongdoing, because they do not realize the intensity of the demands in the unconscious for gratification. It may take serious circumstances to wake them up, such as tragedies, natural disasters, a painful divorce, a death in the family, failure in professional life, breaking a leg, or maybe an addiction, to reveal the depth of the problem. In other words, it takes getting hit over the head by a two-by-four, metaphorically speaking, to recognize that our programs for happiness are not so hot after all.

Once you're thoroughly on the path of transformation, there remains the process of unwinding habits of thinking and over-identification with prepackaged values and preconceived ideas that belong to the socialization period. We don't want to do something that would offend our social group and cause them to reject us since some of our self-identity is drawn from or dependent on the group. This childish phase of growing up needs to be transcended, but many of us don't get to those issues until life itself has bounced us around enough that we realize that we need a power greater than ourselves to help. The sponsor is a window onto that power as someone who can reinforce and encourage us to face the dark side of ourselves. It is painful to recognize just how prone to evil we are capable of being. External circumstances tend to challenge us as to just who we are in a way that ordinary life doesn't, unless you embrace a spiritual program like AA. It is a much more humane way to proceed than by the route of tragedy, disaster, and overwhelming suffering. Many people don't always handle suffering well. It's a tough path and it has to be fully accepted to work. The steps of AA or the contemplative path (or both together) will work if you stick to them.

TS: You often hear at an AA meeting someone saying that they're a grateful alcoholic. I couldn't understand that in the beginning. Alcoholics have gone through so much pain, physical, mental, and spiritual, that they get to the point at which they have no other place to turn; and that's fortunate because the places they were turning to were not good for them. But now when they hit a brick wall, they can't go any further. There's nothing else out there for them. They hit bottom and they reach up, and God and AA are there, and that's so fortunate. Out of the pain comes a spiritual life that is healing.

TK: This is indeed a great insight. What causes God pain, I believe, is not our sins as such (I don't think God is easily offended), but the consequences of our sins that cause us so much pain: humiliation, frustration, guilt for harm done to others. In actual fact, the moment we accept negative feelings, sit with our despair, desolation, hopelessness or frustration, and the overwhelming sense of failure, God takes them all upon Himself, makes them His own, and joins us in our sufferings. As Christians, we believe that this is what Christ does. The acceptance of ourselves just as we are enables God to take all our sufferings and weaknesses to Himself and to transform us. This is inner resurrection, freedom from the bondage of our emotional programs for happiness and over-identification with our social group.

TS: I have a special topic that's near and dear to many alcoholics, and that is fear. It's often labeled *self-centered fear* at AA meetings. When we put down a drink, many of us, if not 100 percent of us, experience fear, even a trembling and uncontrollable fear. For most of us, this fear comes from a source we can only call the unknown, although some have specific fears. Anyway, after our initial recovery, perhaps with the help of medications, we still encounter substantial fears and anxieties, not knowing the source or reason why they occur.

Could you, Father, describe fear and why you think the alcoholic is revisited by it so often and sometimes intensely?

TK: Fear is a problem, not just for alcoholics, but for anybody with a false self. As I said earlier, the false self develops along with the ego as the center of the universe. New experiences are interpreted in relationship to what the ego wants or considers safe, beneficial, and helpful for itself. All the activities of the false self are basically self-centered or selfish.

If you think you are the center of the universe, maybe not explicitly, but act that way, then you have plenty of reason to be afraid. The expectations one has of being able to control one's environment or one's future are total illusions. The mid-life crisis does away with most of them. If that doesn't work, then old age and senility does the rest. And if they don't work, death finally succeeds.

Our emotional programs for happiness are never going to work. That's a basic principle. There's a certain intuitive wisdom in our basic goodness, as the image of God. At a certain level, we're always uneasy with ourselves because we know that what we want to happen and expect to happen is based on expectations that have no basis in reality. They're just part of our syndrome of supporting this illusion with as many gratifications as we can. Through circumstances and personal honesty, these are gradually reduced. There comes a crisis when we have to let go of ourselves as the center of the universe. This is enshrined in AA as the third step that says we turned "our will and our lives over to the care of God." That's the beginning of the undoing of fear. Jesus said in the Gospel that fear is useless. In that context, fear refers to the *emotion* of fear. Sometimes scripture speaks of the fear of God, but that's a technical term that really means to be constantly aware of the presence of God or to have a right relationship with God, which is of course trust, not the emotion of fear. Anything that we bring with us from early life, from our Christian or other education that tends to make God look hazardous or as a punishing God, are childish projections of fear that we need to get rid of. Some AA people who have had a strict religious education have to realize that there are some ideas of God or attitudes toward God that they brought with them from early childhood and never updated as they grew up, and these have to go. Attitudes toward God tinged with the emotion of fear are a hindrance to the spiritual life. They are also a hindrance to the Twelve Steps of AA. These mistaken attitudes toward God are: a tyrant who demands instant obedience, a policeman always on the watch, or a judge always ready to bring down the verdict of guilty, even for thoughts that are inappropriate. A child cannot deal with the distinction between external behavior and thoughts. A strict moral education very often leads to thoughts or feelings about God that are negative, even to the point of thinking of God as hazardous or a kind of monster that you stay away from because, at the slightest misstep, God will plunge us into the depths of hell. Hell is the worst sanction that anybody ever thought up. It's primarily a state of consciousness rather than a place. Some people are in hell in this life. States of utter discouragement that some alcoholics have been through are an analogue of what hell is like. According to the understanding of some theologians, hell may be looked upon as part of the purification process that was not completed while in this world. The spiritual journey is meant to transform us, as the twelfth step says, into God's way of doing things. The illusory big "I" that is our ego becomes the truly big "I am" of God's presence, which is one of love, tenderness, and mercy. It joins us in our human melodrama, whatever that actually is, in order to transform us and through us in redeeming the rest of humanity. The human race is meant to be transformed as a species. The whole human family has the destiny to become God-like. This evolution may take a few more millennia, but is now possible for an individual to attain. God's will is that everyone is to be saved. There's no punishment in God's heart. That's the last thing God thinks about. Whatever hurts in daily life, whatever disappointments and tragedies may overtake us, these are not signs that God doesn't love us, but rather that we are part of a greater plan in which our sufferings are redeeming both for ourselves and for other people in a way beyond our imagination.

The angst that alcoholics suffer as they struggle for sobriety and experience depression is not a punishment. This is painful not because they've done something wrong, but simply because God is moving them to deeper levels of self-surrender. True humility may require us to pass through what seems like ever-recurring failures to overcome our defects. Actually, these very failures are enabling us to grow in humility. When we are finally willing to have our faults corrected by God they will begin to disappear. We need not put ourselves down because it's taking such a long time. We have this pervasive illness called the *human condition*, and it's very deeply rooted. It took years to develop and it's going to take a long time to unwind. This will take place by removing the obstacles in us, that is, our psychological defense mechanisms, the chief of which is thinking too much. The discipline of not thinking (at least deliberately) for a certain period of time every day not only deepens our relationship to God through silence It also is a discipline to help us let go of the contents of the false self as it emerges into awareness.

Fear is the opposite of love. Even more than hatred. When you are afraid, you are not loving. Love is as Paul says in 1 Corinthians 13, the most excellent way. The Twelve Steps partake of that excellent way by changing fear into love. When fear arises, the proper response is to drop it as fast as possible, either by renewing acts of trust or just by ignoring it in your body. Instead of reaching for a pill too quickly, just sit with the sensation and feel the fear. The unconscious evacuates traumatic experiences that have been repressed by feeling them exactly as they were felt at the time that the psyche shoved them into the unconscious. Their intensity was the reason why we buried it. As a result, there's a fear of going through that pain again. But now that we are adults, the same circumstances are not going to affect us the same way. It's the idea that we're going to suffer the same unbearable hurt that makes us reach for distractions or to get away from the anticipated pain by some compensatory activity. If we just sit through it and lap it up and say, "Welcome," God comes to us in the storm. If I just wait out the storm, the presence of God will appear and the troubled waters will become calm.

Fear then, as an emotion, is not us. When we say, "I'm afraid," this is not true. We should rather say, "I have *feelings* of

fear." Once this distinction gets clear in your mind, you realize that feelings can change. The real you is the great "I am,"
the center of our being, the Source from which we emerge,
body, soul, and spirit at every moment, the loving embrace
that keeps us in being all the time and enables us function.
Even sinful action cannot happen without God's help.

We cannot get away from this God. Since God is love,
there's no reason to want to. All the fears we have are based
on illusion, misconceptions of God. If we just keep quiet and
let God be God, we can't help but be reassured. Since our
faults are not going to go away, the best response is to have a
friendly attitude toward them. That is to say, these are means
that teach us how weak we are and how much we depend
on God. So we welcome this further information on that
subject. We don't identify with evil inclinations by carrying
them out. We don't project them on others and say, "they
made me afraid," or "they made me angry." We realize that
we have feelings, but we are not our feelings, and hence God
can change them once we become willing. We have to tell
God often, even when we're not sure it's true, "I am willing
that you take away my faults." This is much more realistic
than to roll up our sleeves and say, "Well, I'm never going to
be angry again." No chance.

TS: In the *24 Hour Book*, I once read that "every fear, worry,
or doubt is disloyalty to God." That ties in so much with what
you just said. And in another place I read that "fear knocked at
the door, faith answered, and there was no one there."

TK: That's very good.

TS: Maybe I should change that to Love now. Love answered and there was no one there. And you also mentioned the act of trust which is very interesting. When fears come, the first act of trust I'll do is perhaps a short prayer. But if it persists, I make a call to my sponsor. I've got to share it, in an act of trust, with another alcoholic. This front line of defense often includes an AA meeting. I go there and often get the right perspective just by listening. It is really being in God's presence because the people are so honest at an AA meeting and I feel prompted to share honestly. The result is the beginning of a healing process. By just getting perspective, I'm halfway home or more, and then of course with God's help and prayer and meditation, that completes the circle.

TK: That's a very beautiful expression of the way to proceed as far as I can see. AA folks need to remember that everybody is in the addictive process. Addiction is the last resort of the psyche to avoid unbearable pain. It is normally so preoccupying that you can't think of the pain. We are all in the addictive process seeking happiness and not knowing where it is to be found. There is only a matter of degree between the average individual and someone in AA. As you know, there are other addictions that carry the message of AA much further than it was originally planned. That's because it speaks to the universal problem in everybody, which is not knowing where true happiness is and looking for it in the wrong places. The pain that follows as a consequence is so great that we need a very strong preoccupation not to think about it, and an addiction meets that need. I venture to say that anybody who lives long enough and who doesn't address the dismantling of the false self will get an addiction of some kind, if they do not have one already.

TS: Over the years, I heard you speak about commentaries and how they build fires under our emotional frustrations. Could we discuss this now and include in your comments ways in which we can guard against them?

TK: I guess this issue calls for a clarification about the relationship between feelings and the imagination. If you think of the human organism as stages of knowing and choosing or knowing, and feeling as the lower stages of consciousness, this is a tri-part brain. There's the reptilian brain, the mammalian brain, and the human brain that has gradually evolved over thousands of years into whatever level of rationality we can now lay claim to. The brain has two parts, the right and the left: one is the basis of rationality and the other of intuition. The intuitive side of the human brain has not been fully developed, at least as much as it could be. The lower level of consciousness, which involves our basic reactions to what we perceive as good or not good, is also linked like the teeth on an old watch so that if one aspect of that level moves, the other one has to move. As soon as you have a feeling, if you don't let it go right away, a commentary, pre-recorded from earlier experiences in life, goes off, and the commentary reinforces the feeling by putting a spin on it that increases its intensity. The new intensity calls for a more radical commentary and these are readily available. There's a constant interaction between feelings and commentaries. For instance, we feel a little bit of irritation. If we don't drop that feeling right away, along comes a commentary that says, "This person shouldn't have done that, maybe they have something against me, maybe they don't like my looks."

The original feeling of irritation then moves to anger, and we think, "What am I going to do about this? I must find some way to get even. I'll criticize him with a double dose of invective." Now the feeling moves on to rage. A further commentary arises that asks, "Why doesn't someone get rid of this person? Better, why doesn't somebody shoot him?"

The emotion takes over so strongly that we're in a temporary state of insanity and the commentary might add, "No, let me break his neck with my bare hands." Then you're in an emotional binge for several hours, days, weeks, and perhaps you never speak to the person again.

Obviously, if you have many of these emotional binges in one day, you'll begin to have some physiological pain. The stronger the emotion, the more it affects the body and sets off the various glands that pour chemicals into the body. These over time can give you a heart attack, a stroke, or other forms of disease. Thus, emotional programs for happiness are actually programs for ill health. What can you do to turn this process off especially if it's very strong? It might be anger in some people or pleasure in somebody else; or it might be anxiety or the fear of never having enough security.

So it is important to realize that the emotions progress in intensity with the help of commentaries. The sooner you drop the initial feeling, the better off you're going to be. Sometimes an insult or something else happens so suddenly that the feelings get out of control right away. But with the help of God, you can notice and recall the damage that you've experienced when they got out of control in the past. As a result when the first movement of irritation comes, there's an equally strong attraction to letting it go.

Some situations or inclinations have to be addressed, they're serious. But most things in everyday life you can drop. A good practice for helping out is to have an active prayer sentence. That is to say, an aspiration that has become so habitual that when a strong reaction arises, so does the new commentary that you've interiorized. By habitual repetition you can store it in the subconscious. One of these aspirations that was used by the Desert Fathers and Mothers was: "Oh God, come to my assistance! Oh Lord, make haste to help me!" They used to say it over and over again all day long when they sat in their hermitages weaving baskets. We can of course select our own aspiration, like: "I put all my trust in You, my God; all my trust is in Your mercy." When the sentence or phrase becomes spontaneous, it erases the old commentaries. If some feeling comes up, we feel it and let it go.

TS: Did you have some further thoughts on aspirations of prayer in regard to commentaries?

TK: When one notices one is getting upset, one can some-times drop the source right away. If one also has at hand an aspiration one has repeated in stray moments—such as wait-ing for the phone to ring or for a bus, or taking a walk, or brushing your teeth, this could provide another way out.

It takes a lot of repetition to establish an aspiration that eventually says itself. If you try such a practice, you need to say the same one over and over again because then there's more chance of it interiorizing. This is only one of a number of ways of dealing with emotions as they arise. The most fundamental principle is that we have feelings but, as noted, we are not our feelings. Hence we don't have to be dominated by them, proj-ect them on others, or act them out. Once we act them out, we only reinforce the vicious cycle of desire, frustration, afflic-tive emotions, commentaries, emotional binges. The whole negative process then creates a greater need for compensation or addictive behavior.

TS: We discussed the topic of humility in step five, but Father Thomas, would you mind commenting on humility as it relates to step seven?

TK: Would you mind repeating step seven at this point?

TS: "Humbly asked Him to remove our shortcomings. . . . "

TK: According to one definition in the Christian tradition, humility is the truth. It is the willingness to accept ourselves just as we are and to be willing that anyone else should know the same facts as well. That's the purpose of sharing them with someone else, like a sponsor who stands for the rest of the human family. When we acknowledge our faults, God immediately can take them away. That's why, I suppose, this step begins with the word "humbly" because it's humility that enables us to be just who we are, whoever we are. If in the present moment our will is turned to God in trust and love, that is all that matters. God doesn't remember the past at all, and that is why whatever we are suffering now is not a punishment, but is simply the natural consequences of the damage we have done to ourselves or others.

Perfect humility goes a step farther than simply the willingness to acknowledge the truth. We are content to be helpless even though our life is unmanageable. But we are also totally willing to be changed. Hence, this attitude might be compared to doing God a favor. In other words, He wants to heal us. We must gently and gratefully acquiesce even though at some secret level we do not want to change. So for love of God and to fulfill his merciful plan for each of us, and for the whole human family, we acknowledge lovingly our weakness; and instead of grousing about it or indulging in self-pity, or getting discouraged by the constant recurrence of our faults, we begin to like them; not that we want to hold on to them, but what we like is the disposition of humility that it engenders, which is a love of the truth that extends even to the truth about our own weakness. As Paul says, "When I am weak, then I am strong." And, "I will only boast of my weakness, so that the power of God may be manifest in me."

Jesus through the parables gives us insights into the heart

of God and the inner nature of the Trinity where everything is gift, where everything is love, and where there is no possessive attitude toward anything.

God the Father is not like any father in this world but father in the sense of the source of all that is.

TS: I just have one remaining question. Some of the fellows I sponsor gave me questions and I just selected one. The question goes like this. In the sixth and seventh steps, AA deals with the dismantling of the false-self system or the removal of character defects. When an individual has been professionally diagnosed with depression or some other mental illness, how can he determine when his suffering comes from the effects of his shortcomings rather than from the clinical aspects of his other disease?

TK: This is a rather nuanced question, isn't it? So the answer has to be nuanced, too.

Depressed feelings are different from a clinical depression. Depressed feelings are usually the result of grief because of circumstances in our lives that deeply frustrate our hopes for happiness. A clinical depression sets off chemical consequences that affect the brain. As a result, clinical depression tends to perpetuate itself. In our time there are drugs that can normalize the chemicals in the brain. One still has the depression, but one is no longer blown away by it. A psychologist can then investigate the basic causes of the depression through psychotherapy.

Contemporary psychotherapists in this country emphasize chemical treatment of depression so much that they don't take the time, when dispositions are normalized, through medication, to investigate the roots of the disorder. Due to the fact that HMOs won't finance lengthy psychotherapy, there may be only 10 or 15 minutes for the psychiatrist or psychotherapist to ask a few basic questions. Patients may get over that period of depression as a result of the medication, but they are liable to fall into another one as long as the sources of it in the unconscious are still in place.

The Twelve Steps have not completed their work because they haven't been supported by a practice of meditation that quiets the mind and disidentifies with the thoughts. Thoughts are one way of preventing primitive emotions, repressed into the unconscious in early childhood, from rising to consciousness. Thinking hides the pain. Through meditation, one makes oneself vulnerable to the undigested emotional material in the unconscious, which then appears as primitive emotions or a bombardment of unwanted thoughts that bear no relationship to the immediate past. That's the signal that these afflictive feelings and thoughts are coming from the unconscious. They almost certainly are if one is in a daily practice of meditation, like centering prayer, in which we deliberately do not think about the thoughts and learn to disregard them. Repressed emotions arise as a result of the body experiencing such deep rest that its defenses go down, and its normal capacity to heal itself manifests in evacuating the repressed thoughts. The unloading of the unconscious is likely to appear during intensive periods of meditation as on a retreat, wherein one meditates for three or four hours a day. We don't recommend that length of time for daily life since it could result in this material coming up too fast, thus causing unnecessary distress or even putting one into a depression. A daily centering prayer practice tends to go at a rate that almost everybody can handle and does its healing work without traumatizing anyone.

A qualified person has to make a distinction between whether one is in a clinical depression or whether one is simply in the depression that is a normal part of the spiritual evolution of unloading the unconscious. The latter involves special periods of purification, which St. John of the Cross has called the night of sense and the night of spirit. These are particular treatments appropriate for certain phases of the spiritual journey in people who are committed to the practice of meditation. In centering prayer, one is simply offering one's whole being to God without reflection, including self-reflection or particular expectations. The purpose of the night of sense is to dismantle the emotional programs for happiness that we brought with us from early childhood involving excessive demands for security, affection, and control through the peace, the sense of being loved by God, and that everything is okay, which arise during the meditative process.

Jesus recommends in Matthew 6:6 entering our inner room, closing the door, and praying to the Father in secret. By this he means moving off the ordinary psychological level of awareness with its tumult and noise and quieting the mind so that one can access the spiritual level of one's being. The movement of the will to consent to God's presence and action relativizes our former view of what happiness is through the affirmation of our basic goodness that accompanies the prayer. As a result the level of trust in God increases, and one is able to bear the unwinding of the false self with its programs for happiness that don't work. The natural result of losing something we counted on is grief. We usually go through a period of mourning, which is not a clinical depression, but simply the natural reaction of losing something we love. When the period of mourning is over, we will experience a new relationship with God, ourself, and everything else. This is vastly more reassuring and refreshing than the exercise of the false self that is constantly overwhelmed by frustration and consequent afflictive emotions.

The false self experiences two things in the course of the unfolding of daily life: exaltation if you get what you want through the gratification of one of the three emotional programs for happiness; or depression when you do not get them and feel frustration. In the latter case, you are a sitting duck for a clinical depression.

In Bill W.'s case, as I understand it from his correspondence with his Jesuit priest friend, Father Dowling, he wrote that he had a depression for twelve years that he couldn't get out of no matter how hard he tried. One day he got the insight that he had an enormous attachment to pleasing other people. This is obviously rooted in the program for affection, esteem, and approval. As soon as he recognized it as the root cause of his depression, he recovered. So deep was his unconscious attachment to that program for happiness from his earliest years that it took him all that time to contact its naked reality and to become humble enough to face it. As soon as he faced and accepted it, he came out of the depression.

Alcoholics need to realize that underneath their addiction to alcohol is this deeper problem that they have to work on. Otherwise, after sobriety, they may turn up with another addiction, or they are in danger of falling back into the one they had. Hence, the importance of cultivating steps six and seven, which is the willingness to be healed of our faults. The three emotional programs for happiness are the three faults that are the root cause of physical, mental, and spiritual poor health. It is like healing the root of a tree rather than just clipping off a few dead leaves or branches that are rotten. The tree's tendency to produce bad fruit will continue until the roots of the tree are healed. The diseased roots of our inner tree are the excessive energy that we put into finding happiness through the gratification of unlimited and unreal demands for the symbols in the culture of affection/esteem/approval, power/control, and safety/security.

These are the issues that we need to deal with in talking to our sponsor, and the sponsor needs to be alert that this problem has to be faced, and then nudge the sponsee into recognizing what the chief attachment is. Usually one of the three predominates, depending on one's temperament and genetic factors. An aggressive person is likely to be interested in power and control issues. Timid souls will be worried about their security needs. Movie stars and athletes are going to be worried about their fame and reputation. They might get thousands of letters praising their performance, yet if they get one letter that says their last movie or last game was lousy, they go into a big depression and have to go to rehab for a month in order to recover from what they feel was an unbearable insult. It wasn't unbearable. It was their thoughts and feelings that were unbearable. That is why we need to be detached from our thinking processes and realize that while the reflective apparatus is a great value in working with life, it has limitations and cannot relate adequately to God by itself. God is the God of infinite mercy and prefers to deal with us at that level. Hence, the more weak and helpless we feel, the more apt we are for the divine concern, because the nature of mercy is to reach out to help those in need. If there were nobody in need, God would have nothing to do. So you're doing him a favor by providing him with enough misery to occupy his infinite power. There's a certain humor in this situation. God doesn't expect us to succeed all the time; He expects us to stumble and fall like little children. If we are humble, it doesn't hurt. But if you have big pretensions, then when you fall down, you might break a few bones.

TS: When someone suspects that he is clinically depressed, would you suggest that he look for someone in the medical profession who is very familiar with the spiritual journey that you're describing?

TK: Absolutely. Even if psychiatrists are not always the most spiritual people, they can be good therapists. There are symptoms of a clinical depression that they can usually pick up. Occasionally, a therapist might judge merely depressed feelings as a clinical depression. Of course, it would be desirable that the therapist have a sense that someone on the spiritual journey is likely to have these depressed feelings without a clinical depression. They would be better qualified to make the diagnosis. If one is in the night of spirit, which is a very profound purification of the unconscious, one might seem to be so depressed and in such agony that he or she needs medication. However, there are cases in which medication may not do any good. It might be better just to say over and over the active prayer sentence: "I put all my trust in you, my God. All my hope is in your mercy."

THE CONNECTIVITY OF STEPS SIX, SEVEN, AND ELEVEN

STEP SIX
Were entirely ready to have God remove all these defects of character.

STEP SEVEN
Humbly asked Him to remove our shortcomings.

STEP ELEVEN
Sought through prayer and meditation to improve our conscious contact with God as we understood Him, praying only for knowledge of His will for us and the power to carry that out.

Tom S.: At the end of the sixth step Bill W. wrote, "We shall have to come to grips with some of our worst character defects and take action toward their removal as quickly as we can."

When I completed step seven, I knew I had done it imperfectly. I still had my character defects deeply in place, but something new was present. You mentioned this before. My attitude toward God was changing. I saw that only He could release me from the paralyzing grip of my character defects.

All of the steps are important, but today I understand more than ever the linkage between steps seven and eleven. As we access God's healing power through prayer and meditation in the eleventh step, I think the walls of our character defects become more evident and then they begin to crumble.

Father Thomas, will you give us your comments regarding prayer and meditation, and the linkage to the healing of our character defects?

Thomas Keating: There is a powerful connection between the two. You have several points in your exposition that deserve comment, but I will focus on what you asked specifically at the end. The practice of prayer, and especially meditation, which is a movement of prayer beyond mere external words, involves not just thinking, but also the affective side of our nature. In other words, meditation in its beginning stages involves finding a certain nourishment, benefit, or profit in reflecting on God as presented in the sacred scriptures. Certainly it would be one of the things to look into in order to get acquainted with God. As our feelings begin to change toward God and we experience the goodness of God, we begin to want to respond to the beauty, the truth, and the goodness revealed in the writings about God or serious reflections about the Ultimate Reality. We now have a new motivation that is backed up by positive feelings that balance off the negative feelings that we had in the past. So when that meditation advances to a place beyond thinking, we are ready to change and it does not seem so hard anymore.

We want to be like God. We want to respond to this goodness. It resonates with our true self, which is our basic goodness. This is an important point. Meditation awakens the realization not only of our faults and weaknesses, but also of our basic goodness. The whole psyche wants to respond to this new awakening of our relationship with God. At the same time, we have the increasing sense of our weakness to do so under our own power, because our habits of behavior that are negative are deeply set and also because we like some of our faults. We would just as soon God would not heal, because we are not quite sure we are ready.

St. Augustine in his *Confessions* wrote about his sexual struggles as a youth. At the time of his conversion, he experienced the tension of wanting to be free of his sexual urges and at the same time not feeling quite ready to give them up. He writes of his dilemma saying, "Oh, God, please save me from these sexual excesses, but not yet." What does "not yet" mean? A few weeks from now, a few years from now? St. Augustine's *Confessions* have resonated down the years because he describes so poignantly the way people feel.

To sum up, we want to be healed and don't want to be healed at the same time. The confrontation becomes more unbearable until finally we say, "If I really want to deepen this relationship, I have to let go of my faults." So we try, but still don't succeed.

The effort to overcome our faults gradually persuades us that our life is unmanageable, because with the best of intentions, we cannot do it. Because I know I can't do it, I ask

God to take them away. The pain of not succeeding becomes a cry for help that is totally sincere. It is the cry for help that pierces the clouds.

The only prayer you need to say is, "Help!" It's right to the point. It describes what we need. And when it comes from a heart that is broken by its own failures, it moves God to the very roots of the divine nature and God responds. It is not a question of forgiveness, because He has already forgiven us as soon as we want to change, but to give us the ability to be free of the straitjacket of the emotional programs for happiness based on those instinctual needs.

The expression of them, since we relied on them and hoped to find happiness through satisfying those needs in the symbols of the culture, are hard to give up. Even when you decide to give them up, you can't. It is in that place that one becomes humble and when one prays, one gets the results.

TS: You know what I notice in AA, too, the concept of sponsorship is so important because the sponsee often does not see his or her own spiritual growth. And they often are very hard on themselves. So the sponsor has to be very close to the sponsee and let him or her know that they are changing and that the goodness at their center is beginning to show.

TK: It is important to emphasize that because deep prayer, especially centering prayer, follows Jesus' formula in Matthew 6:6, which reads, "If you want to pray, enter your inner room, close the door, and pray to your *Abba*, in secret." *Abba* is the Aramaic word for a loving father. The father, Jesus concludes, "who sees in secret will reward you." In the inner room two things are happening. One is the affirmation of our basic goodness. In Christian terms it is the fact that we are created in the image of God, and this goodness can never be lost by any amount of misbehavior. It is always there. It is God's permanent gift to us. Even though it is covered over by layers of psychological damage and misbehavior, it can always revive. You just have to give it the chance to express itself by reducing the obstacles.

TS: At AA we just take off one piece of junk at a time and it seems to work.

TK: There is nothing greater than to release the activity of our true self, the self that manifests the goodness of God in our particular uniqueness.

DEPRESSION, PSYCHOTHERAPY, AND DIVINE THERAPY

TS: I have got one final question. Over the years I have noticed people with time in AA still have problems with fear and insecurity, maybe low self-esteem. I should not be surprised by that because Bill Wilson experienced it with twelve years of depression from 1944 to 1955. As you know, he wrote an article in 1958 called "The Next Frontier: Emotional Sobriety." In there he said in the first sentence, I think many AA "oldsters" still find they often lack emotional sobriety. Some in AA—this is my own comment—run for the local therapist when they are faced with depression, but it occurs to me that we often have not given the divine therapist, or God, the time or attention necessary to work his miracle of recovery. Could you comment, Father Thomas, on the interplay of these therapists?

TK: This, of course, depends a lot on the circumstances. If the person is in a clinical depression, he or she needs to be treated medically because there are now medications that can be taken to heal or at least to balance the psyche that is in depression. You cannot really give psychotherapy until the force of the clinical depression has been reduced. In other words, depression does not go anywhere. It goes around in circles. Chemically, it seems that it tends to reinforce itself. So without medication, you cannot get the brain back to an attitude that can be open to investigate the causes in the unconscious of the depression in the first place. If you just take chemicals, all that you cure are the symptoms.

Many therapists are set up for just chemical treatment of mental disorders, especially depression. It is true, psychotherapy is very expensive and usually long. But just to treat it chemically is to give up trying to cure it and it simply enables the person to live a little more comfortable life with the same problems. The causes of depression are not going to go away through chemicals. Someone who is on a spiritual path, such as AA, has the special influence of the divine therapist. Grace is working.

When a depression comes, one can certainly look for

professional help if it is enlightened and if it accepts the spirituality of the situation. The spirituality is solely up to the
person being treated, as well as the possibility of the divine
grace acting in that person. Without that view of a person's
psychic life, I would not recommend a psychiatrist because
they are not treating the whole person. They are only treating the body and the brain with chemicals. They may even
think of a human being as a mere juxtaposition of chemicals. That would work if we were automatons of some kind;
but according to religious experience over centuries and
especially mystical experiences of the spirituality of the soul
and God, this position is really unscientific. Science can now
prove empirically that meditation changes the chemistry of
the brain for the better. There are excellent psychotherapists.
The ideal would be a synthesis between a sponsor, a therapist,
and the sponsee, in which they all work together to help the
afflicted person each in his or her own way.

Sometimes counseling can lead to a breakthrough in
understanding that reinforces the work of grace. Grace does
not normally speak in words, but rather in attitudes, attractions, and inspirations. There is no inherent conflict between
psychology and the spiritual nature of the client. It is just that
the work of the divine therapist goes much further and much
deeper.

The purpose of ordinary psychotherapy, as I understand
it, is to help a person lead a normal life when he or she
is hampered by psychological problems. The purpose of the
divine therapy is the healing of the roots of all our problems

and to transform our attitudes and, indeed, the whole of our human nature into the mind and heart of Christ. In other words, to introduce us though grace into the interior life of God. This involves a transformation of our attitudes, faculties, and bodies so that we can receive the maximum amount of the transmission of divine life that is possible given the limits of human nature. The Fathers of the church who wrote about this subject called this process *deification*. In other words, the purpose of this journey, even the Twelve Steps of AA, is not just to become a better person and to maintain recovery, as important as these are. It is to change us into the divine way of being human. This is a much bigger and more comprehensive project and opens us to the full extent of human possibilities and capacities. You cannot do much better than to become God by participation.

The divine therapy goes much further than psychotherapy. Psychotherapy can be a kind of handmaid of the spiritual journey and enrich it. It supports the work of grace in particular circumstances that may need psychological counseling or be helped by it. Actually a sponsor is doing a lot of psychological counseling whether you call it that or not, or whether the sponsor is fully qualified with a degree. He or she is really addressing the psychological problems of the sponsee. In the course of that service, it may happen that psychological problems arise that are so serious that the sponsee clearly needs professional help.

One of these problems, of course, is abuse. Sexual abuse, for example, causes enormous emotional harm in a child whose emotional life is not ready for that kind of experience. Its future capacity to relate to other people in an intimate way may be harmed, irreparably in some cases, unless it goes through the kind of counseling that psychotherapy can offer in this area that supports them in their healing process. The child often feels guilty regarding sexual abuse, especially if it is a question of incest, which places the child in a double bind. Its whole security system depends on its maintaining relationships to its parent. Now the parent has become for them a painful experience. The child needs both the love of the parent and respect for its physical boundaries, which are being disregarded. If it has negative and positive messages coming at it at the same time, its emotional life is cast into chaos. The child has to find ways of coping with this situation. One way could be the repression of all sexual expression and this may render it incapable of an intimate sexual relationship. This is not an area with which an average sponsor is equipped to deal. It may be necessary to suggest that the victim get professional help in looking into the emotional consequences of the tragedy.

There are also other situations that could be helped by a period of counseling. A low self-image, sense of rejection, being unloved, these can be healed by the divine therapist, but sometimes God expects us to make use of other means. Or at least by doing so, it could speed up the process and support it.

TS: I relate so much to what you said. When I was drinking I sought the help of a doctor. I sought the help of a priest. I sought the help of a psychologist and I was not getting the help I needed. When I came into AA, I got the help I needed from another alcoholic because he was healing in all three areas. He was addressing all three areas, physical, emotional, and spiritual. That is what I needed. AA is such an inspired program. It led me into a change of life and then into a spiritual life.

TK: Yes, I think that AA is such a well-thought-out and experiential program that addresses the whole person—body, soul, and spirit—that it can do without a lot of psychological help. Unless you are in a spiritual program like AA, the interrelatedness of body, soul, and spirit are sometimes piecemeal. To work on one without the others is not as effective, or at least it is slow going. AA is so full of wisdom that it normally meets the ordinary needs for most people arising from damage in early childhood.

To get back to an earlier thing that you were saying when you were quoting Bill Wilson and his depression, this seems to me to be a very interesting experience. He, as the founder of AA, has a special symbolic value. I think he says in his experience maybe that half of the people in recovery after a certain number of years go through a depression. As you said, his lasted a dozen years. That is a long time.

The question is why after experiencing the freedom and grace of recovery, and going through the steps as thoroughly as he did, would you fall into a depression? It may be that there is something else that is not fully addressed even in the AA program, which is probably there and it is there, in my view, in the eleventh step, which is the regular practice of prayer and meditation, especially meditation in the sense of non-conceptual meditation and cultivating interior silence at the spiritual level of our being. Thinking more than anything else conceals like a manhole cover the unconscious and its contents. When you take off the cover, the contents or the odor of the contents will emerge to consciousness, and most people will quickly put the cover back on.

No one enjoys the feelings of moral corruption that are stored in the unconscious. In the concrete, it is stored in the body which is the warehouse for the undigested emotional material of a whole lifetime. We have to acknowledge that as our own and to face it, feel it, give it to God, and then it is gone.

BILL W.'S DEPRESSION AND THE HEALING OF THE UNCONSCIOUS

TS: About Bill's depression and why it happened, could you give us a few more comments on that?

TK: This is an important paradigm for people in AA. If it happened to the founder, it could happen to anybody. In one of his letters to Father Dowling, Bill W. writes about his depression, and he says that one day he realized that he had an enormous investment in pleasing people, that is, in being acceptable to everyone. The next day he was cured of the depression. That is what he says.

I was especially struck with this because it responds to my understanding of how the three basic instincts of the child work once they are fossilized into energy centers around the instinctual needs of security, power and control, affection and esteem. The latter is what Bill W. calls *prestige*. This emotional energy center was hidden from him until the moment when in some way he realized there was more work to be done and he was open to this deeper revelation.

What he is really saying is that his basic problem was not alcohol, but underlying that addiction was the need for approval. His desire for prestige was so strong that when it was frustrated or in danger of being frustrated, it sent him into a depression. A depression for some people may be less painful than facing the pain of their more fundamental investment in one of the three energy centers that are secretly controlling their deepest motivation. Hence, their unconscious is constantly responding to this hidden fear or pain that alcohol successfully covers up. So of course do other addictions. The investment in one of those energy centers sets off what might be called the addictive process. The course of action that leads to an addiction is the last stage of trying to avoid the pain.

Letting go of attachment to finding happiness in one of those three basic instinctual needs is the radical road to recovery and human health. The insight enables us to see what the real problem is. When we let go, there is no more pain. But until we let go, the pain is strong while its source remains hidden from us. When the pain is intolerable, any-body can fall into an addiction of some kind. The eleventh step prepares the recovering alcoholic to become vulnerable to the roots of his or her unconscious where the problem really is, the problem that is deeper than the addiction to alcohol.

When that is resolved, one moves to the twelfth step and is transformed into inner freedom, peace, joy, and the fruits of the Spirit, which are meekness, gentleness, unselfish love, joy, peace, goodness, self-control, all of the things that are part of our true self, with its basic goodness that now is free to express itself.

It is not enough, therefore, to achieve recovery from alcohol. One also has to recover from the addictive process. The steps of AA are thus relevant to every human being, because they are a remedy for what is the basic affliction of the human family. Religious circles have called this basic affliction the Fall and Original Sin. The fact is recognized universally in all religions.

Something is very wrong with human nature, although human nature in its basic creation is very good. So this is what spiritual life is all about. Life is about trying to resolve this extraordinary double bind. It is not a question of per-sonal sin. Not a question, therefore, of punishment. The heal-ing process that sometimes feels so painful is simply taking the necessary medication or therapy, and the unconscious is scared to death that it is going to be more painful. This is only because it has the illusion that it would find happiness, if it could get away with it, in any program in the culture that might provide gratification for the outlandish demands and unreal expectations we have for security, power and control, and affection and esteem.

This is the universal problem. Within that insight, the AA program, if it is limited only to recovery from alcohol, is not enough to take away the deepest source of the problem.

We don't meet reality where it is or accept other people as they are unless they fulfill our censorship of whether they will feed into our need for whatever our emotional program happens to be foremost at the time. This is an area that psychotherapy pursues but does not go far enough. I don't think even the Twelve Steps of AA pursue it consciously or directly. It is certainly implied in the eleventh and twelfth steps, actually throughout the steps. This openness to turning our life over to God certainly implies the ultimate surrender, which is the surrender of the unconscious and whatever is there.

The human condition is nobody's fault. It is the way things are. We grow up without the experience of the divine presence and, hence, we look for happiness somewhere else. This becomes a habit that is very hard to let go of as long as our false self develops ways of dealing with the frustration of our instinctual needs.

TS: I thought, too, while you were sharing, that Bill Wilson had a habit of quick recoveries. He had a sudden spiritual awakening, and now we talk about his recovery overnight.

For most of us, the troops, so to speak, we might have to add recovery *with patience* because it is God's timetable, not ours.

TK: People respond differently to the awakening of grace within them. It is striking that it took him twelve years of suffering to come to that point.

STEP EIGHT

Made a list of all persons we had harmed, and became willing to make amends to them all.

Tom S.: Bill Wilson defined "harmed" as the "result of instincts in collision which caused physical, mental, emotional, or spiritual damage to people." Father Thomas, how do we spiritually damage other people?

Thomas Keating: All harm on any level is spiritual harm because spiritual harm strikes at what is the source of human health. Namely, a spirit that is open, free, loving, and concerned. All the things that are most valuable and rich in human life have their source in the spirit. So if the spirit is damaged, then to that degree, all of us suffer in some degree.

TS: In looking at the relationship between the alcoholic parent and the child, I can see how you could apply that and how the child is spiritually damaged because of the absence of spiritual guidance, education, and so forth.

TK: The health of any relationship relies on being able to bring one's total presence to the other person or to the group that one is relating to, whether this is God or other people, or even oneself or the rest of creation.

So if, as I understand it, in an alcoholic problem, one is not present to other people when one is under the influence of alcohol, so the child experiences the parent in different ways. Sometimes he is pleasant, sometimes unpleasant. This ambiguity gives the child a sense of great insecurity because the parent is the chief source of security in a child's life, especially an infant's life. So if the parent is one thing one day and another thing another day, or is one thing this time of the day and a later time of the day is a totally different person because they are under the influence of alcohol, this is extremely unsettling for the child, at least as I understand the literature on the subject. I came from a family where, at least when I left at the age of twenty, we did not have any alcoholics.

TS: My father was an alcoholic. Because we look at alcoholism as a disease today, I can understand how the diseased one, or the alcoholic, does unintentionally pass on bad habits and so forth to his children. But fortunately, God is there to pick up the pieces eventually. At least that happened in my situation.

TK: He is always picking up the pieces. There are plenty of them for most of us whether you are an alcoholic or not.

TS: Bill Wilson mentioned that no field of investigation can be more fruitful in improving our relationships than this detailed list of persons we have harmed and our willingness to make amends. But there are obstacles. He wrote about the obstacles to step eight. Four of them, actually. The first one, which Mary Mrozowski, one of the founders of Contemplative Outreach, spoke about often, is forgiveness. It seems in making our amends they are fairly shallow if we don't first forgive the person for harms done to us. I wonder, Father, if you could speak a little about the concept of forgiveness and how important it is to feel from the heart, before we move on to amends.

TK: Just to make it clear so I understand whose forgiveness you are talking about, are you talking about the alcoholic forgiving somebody else? Or the person they have victimized in some degree forgiving them?

TS: That is a good point. We make a list of the people to whom we want to make amends for what we have done. But often a person on the list will have harmed us.

In order to make amends, heartfelt amends, what Bill Wilson is suggesting is that we forgive them first for any harm they have done us. Then we can make our amends because if we don't do that, the amends may be tainted by our resentments.

TK: If we are trying to make amends to someone whom we feel offended by or persecuted by, it is not going to be easy, or it will be superficial or halfhearted. So maybe you have to postpone the amends until you have, to the best of your ability, forgiven them from the heart. That does not mean there will not still be some feelings of hurt, but I would think it best to try to make amends when one has some control over those hurt feelings, otherwise the amends might go awry. They might be misunderstood and the other person might think you are manipulating them.

TS: Some of these resentments are so deep-seated. Would you say that perhaps praying for the other person or something like that might be helpful?

TK: That is at least a good place to begin. As I understand it, in the process of forgiveness, there are certain steps and, of course, the steps are bigger in the degree or the depth that one felt offended, abused, or hurt. When you think of the damage that is done by having lived for a long time under oppressive circumstances, forgiveness, at least as a genuine feeling, is going to be virtually impossible. The most you can do is to make a bare act of will, saying, "I forgive the guy." But there is no feeling to back it up. One needs to go through the steps of forgiveness, one of which is to recognize how resentful one is of the other person, how angry one is, and to deal with those feelings; allowing them to come to consciousness, feeling them, perhaps sharing them with somebody, and getting counseling that would help one deal with the intensity of those feelings. Beyond anger, there is often a profound sense of grief. It is only when those or similar feelings dealt with and have been expressed, not to the person, but to someone else, that the intensity of the feeling level diminishes and one can reach a point at which forgiveness as a genuine feeling is possible.

The intention is to forgive, yes. But if it is going to be a genuine reconciliation, one has to pass through the steps of forgiveness. And that involves handling one's resentments. That may take quite a while. I think we need to recognize the intensity of our resentments. Resentments that we don't face tend to turn into guilt feelings.

There has to be an easing of the intensity of the emotions. Prayer would help to do that, but it would take some time. So out of zeal for the steps, to rush out right away to make amends would be dangerous, as Bill Wilson evidently foresaw. Perhaps he experienced it.

It is better to act with prudence under the guidance of the sponsor and even seek professional help that might warn us that we are not ready to engage in any face-to-face reconciliation yet.

Suppose somebody has shot one of your children. This is an enormous tragedy to go through because the immediate human response is anger and revenge. How to get even, how to get justice, especially if one's child was completely innocent. It requires heroic determination and struggle to forgive from the heart.

TS: We have so many examples of that today. Someone once said that resentments are like bars on a prison. We are the one in jail, but forgiveness melts the bars.

TK: Yes. That is very good.

TS: And sets us free. I think forgiveness is freedom, actually.

TK: There is no doubt it is the path to health, freedom, and peace, but the emotions that are deeply hurt will not let you do that until they have been in some way laid to rest. I can think of one or two classical experiences of forgiveness that took years to accomplish fully, but once they were accomplished, they did enormous good, not only to themselves, but to the original perpetrator and to even people who just heard the story.

TS: I think of the one where the Pope had visited that fellow that tried to assassinate him.

TK: That is a classical example of forgiveness. Sometimes it is easier to forgive offenses to ourselves than to someone whom we greatly love or were responsible for.

TS: One of the other obstacles that Bill wrote about was "fear of face-to-face admissions" in step nine. We often have to remind our sponsees that the eighth step only requires a list. Some amends in step nine cannot be made or should not be made.

TK: Step eight is basically an exercise in honesty with oneself in making a list of all that one has done. It is an exercise of self-knowledge. Then what you do after that is subject to the norms of common sense and whether making amends would be effective or make the situation worse.

TS: Right. Tied in with this is something that Bill Wilson called purposeful forgetting, denials that we ever really harmed anyone. We often rationalize our own behavior.

TK: Or maybe how much we harmed somebody. Maybe

you recognize that we did slap somebody in the face, but we forget that we knocked out his two front teeth and nearly choked the guy. Sure, honesty is important in self-knowledge. It is emphasized in the steps, but it is also essential to a good confession. As you know, in the sacrament of reconciliation you are supposed to reflect on what you have done before you go in. The idea is to avoid the unconscious tendency to cover up the seriousness of some of the stuff that we have done. It's not much fun to tell a priest even in a dark confessional about something one might have done. So this is a good exercise in genuine honesty without any holds barred. I presume having passed through the seven earlier steps you would be ready to do that.

TS: I guess we could pray for honesty when we are doing the step. One of the other obstacles that Bill Wilson mentioned is the emotional conflicts that exist below the level of consciousness, which you may be familiar with.

TK: These are the levels that interest me the most, because this is our secret motivation. Another word for it would be the *dynamics* of the unconscious, that is to say, the various things that we repressed that were emotionally traumatic to us in early life, the energy of which remains in the unconscious, and hence not known to us, and can secretly influence our decisions even in very important matters like marriage or a religious vocation.

TS: Or making a list of people we had harmed.

TK: Yes. Absolutely.

TS: I guess there is nothing much that can be done about these emotional conflicts at such deep levels at this point. I am thinking of the interconnectedness of the steps, how we do the eighth step imperfectly and make the list. We do the ninth step and make the direct amends, but it is really not until we get to the eleventh step that we begin to heal at deep levels.

TK: I think Twelve Steppers, if it is not too flip a term, should know that in serious meditation, especially non-conceptual meditation or prayer when one is simply being in the presence of God and consenting to God's presence and action within, it is precisely the deep rest that comes from trusting God and experiencing the affirmation of our basic goodness that often accompanies the beginnings of a meditation practice. As a first step, it reduces the defense mechanisms in the unconscious. As these relax, the actual contents of the unconscious, such as the intensity of our resentment or anger, begin to come to our awareness. We may then realize that this emotion or mindset is a lot more serious than we thought and that there is a lot more at stake than we ever realized. This helps us to understand how we act out, in daily life, emotional needs that were hidden from us, which are now beginning to come to consciousness through the process of meditation.

There is only a certain level of honesty you can reach in the eighth step until you have moved into the eleventh and practice that a while. Then when you go through the steps and go back and look at eight, it is going to be a very different eight.

A whole new world opens up. This is where, to face it courageously, one needs a relationship with God that is not one of fear, but of trust, that God is going to help us face these issues, and make amends that God thinks are appropriate. These will have a significant beneficial effect for ourselves and for those we might have wounded.

TS: The sponsor has an important part to play here. He or she is the one that encourages the sponsee or the alcoholic to keep going because the sponsor knows as we accomplish each additional step, that the healing is going to permeate right back to the other steps and at a deeper level. Bill Wilson also wrote, in the investigation of our relationships we can go "far beyond those things which were superficially wrong with us to see those flaws which were basic. Flaws which were sometimes responsible for the whole pattern of our lives." I guess that really ties into what you just said.

TK: And to be more specific, those patterns are basically rooted in the three instinctual needs of human nature necessary for survival as the infant. These are basic patterns of conduct that we need to get clear about. In the course of growing up they fossilized into energy centers in which we poured a lot of energy in order to obtain gratification or satisfaction in one of those three areas.

The normal result of the activity of these energy centers

is that we experience more frustration in them as they get more unrealistic, unlimited, and demanding on other people. The latter are not going to acquiesce to our outrageous demands. All our relational problems are basically rooted in our exaggerated demands that everyone should respect our need for security, however unreasonable and unlimited, and hence, unattainable. We may even think there is something wrong with other people if they do not provide what we have come to expect as a strict right.

Look at any advertising. It always appeals to one of the first three energy centers and sometimes to the other major foundation of the false self, which is over-identification with one's group. We tend to draw our identity from the values of our group and acquiesce to them for fear of being rejected or left out.

TS: Thank you, Father. This concludes our step eight discussion.

STEP NINE

Made direct amends to such people wherever possible, except when to do so would injure them or others.

Tom S.: Before making amends, Bill W. suggests that we consult with our "sponsor or spiritual advisor, particularly in grave areas." This is the first time that Bill uses the term spiritual advisor in the steps, to my knowledge. Father Keating, would you comment on the benefits of a spiritual advisor and how such an advisor could interact with a sponsor?

Thomas Keating: A spiritual advisor is a kind of sponsor. Aren't they the same?

TS: In this particular step he is referring to a spiritual advisor.

TK: He is referring to an additional advisor?

TS: Yes. I found in my own case even today I have an AA sponsor, but I use someone else for the deep spiritual advice that I need on a day-to-day basis. Some people use a sponsor for everything. Others feel that they need a spiritual advisor.

TK: It depends on the qualifications of the sponsor. He does not have to be spiritually trained person. But every bit of qualification is certainly a boon, especially for anyone who is seriously trying to negotiate the steps, because they are likely to get into the spiritual levels of relating to God and other people from the word *go*.

The need increases as you negotiate the steps. So I think it would be helpful to have a spiritual guide. The sponsor is important because the sponsor is focused on the steps and is available on short notice. If I'm not mistaken, that is part of the agreement between the two.

Spiritual guides, if they are really good, are very busy people. They are hard to get, hard to track down even on the phone. They are called to do many other services. They also have any number of other clients that are trying to get their advice, too. Perhaps it is better to use them for more serious things that would require special qualifications that an ordinary sponsor would not necessarily have. So, sure, to have both would be a blessing.

The main thing is to be open with someone who has some experience and who is trustworthy. Then the degree of qualifications only makes the person more desirable.

TS: I think you once referred to the divine therapist. Perhaps that is the best advisor we can have, God Himself. But that still requires some action on our own to develop that relationship with God.

TK: It would be helpful, too, to have a guide in addition to your sponsor and the spiritual director, because when you get into the higher steps of AA, I suspect you may experience the symptoms of interior purification that are characteristic of the divine therapy, especially interior struggles with a backwash of guilt feelings, shame, and humiliation.

This trial is like being in hell for some people. In fact, it is hell, if by hell you mean a psychological state of desolation, loneliness, boredom, alienation, and despair that often accompanies trying to recover from some addiction. Hence, the benefit of advice that recognizes the various elements in one's suffering can be helpful in suggesting the proper remedies.

TS: I know for myself, in the beginning I had a great sponsor. He helped me in all three areas, actually, the physical, mental, and spiritual. But there came a point where I went back to church, so to speak, and I got in touch with a priest in my parish and we started to delve more into the spiritual area where I felt a need.

I ran into fellows in other religions that found the same thing. Their spiritual advisors seemed to work together with their sponsors in a fashion. But some don't need the spiritual advisor I guess.

I just raise this point because the first time I saw it was in step nine. Bill also suggests that we earnestly seek God's help and guidance before proceeding. Can you give us some suggestions on how that can be accomplished?

TK: You might make a short retreat in which you review the list of people that you need to make amends to and give more time to prayer. In the silence or solitude of a retreat one's thoughts tend to clarify, or at least they are not interfered with by distractions coming from everyday life, such as the phone ringing, the television or radio blasting, people chatting, and traffic noise.

TS: I often suggest that the sponsee say a prayer before approaching the other person on the day of the amends.

TK: By all means. To make amends one needs all the help one can get.

TS: There are times, though, that a sponsee, when he is in the course of making direct amends, meets with bitterness and humiliating responses from the person to whom the direct amends is offered. What spiritual reassurance comes to mind, Father, in those situations to overcome the resulting discouragement of the sponsee?

TK: I would go back to the sponsor and tell him, "I was covered with burning coals of indignation and I took off as fast as I could. What is the next step?"

I think the next step would be to postpone any further dealing with the issue for the time being and try to recover from the sense of failure. It is important to realize that the effort itself was a success. How it actually turned out is secondary.

In God's eyes, every effort is a success. Even if everyone thinks it was a total flop, including ourselves, despite appearances some good may have been done.

Maybe the other person, after thinking it over, will see things differently and be moved to appreciate the generosity of the gesture. Who knows? But if the decision is to make amends, go through with it and leave the results to God. If it is not accepted, you did the best you could, and so move on to the next person on your list.

TS: In effect, we are responsible for the effort, not the result.

TK: Exactly.

TS: It's true what Bill W. said: We shall need the following qualities to make direct amends: "good judgment, a careful sense of timing, courage, and prudence." I guess underlying that would be a strong or a deep relationship with a loving Higher Power. I think that is key in this approach, the strong relationship with a loving God. Do you have any thoughts on that?

TK: This would help those four recommendations of Bill W. to have their maximum effect. All four of them are excellent recommendations. Translating them into convictions would be one of the fruits of prayer. It could give one greater courage to follow them out.

But again, as I listen over and over to the Twelve Step program, I keep thinking that if people would develop the eleventh step a little sooner, it could help them negotiate some of the earlier steps. But not being a member of AA, I don't feel qualified to offer anything more than a suggestion for consideration by those who are experienced in this area.

TS: We really don't wait until the eleventh step to introduce prayer and meditation. In the third step we turn our will and our life over to God.

TK: That is a great prayer.

TS: I guess that is the main prayer. We constantly go back to that as we hit stumbling blocks in the other steps.

TK: I would like to clarify more precisely what my suggestion was. It was not just to offer any prayer, but specifically the kind of practice that centering prayer represents, in which one is not thinking about God so much as communing with God, cultivating interior silence, and letting go of thoughts, at least in one's intention. This practice helps to clear the mind of the kind of mental chatter that makes centering prayer seem so difficult.

TS: It is very interesting you said that. A couple years ago in Scarsdale, New York, we started an eleventh step meditation meeting where we sit in silence for twenty minutes just in God's presence. Some of the people coming into that meeting are in early sobriety; and yet they enjoy it very much. They feel somehow spiritually refreshed as a result of the silent meditation.

I never discourage any person, even a newcomer, from going to that meeting. For some people, they need the beginner's meetings more than the eleventh step meeting, of course. But it does not seem to do anyone any harm in going and just to sit in God's presence for twenty minutes.

TK: It is not going to do anyone any harm. But what it may do, without our realizing it, is introduce us to a spiritual dimension, or at least, a quasi-experience, that alerts us to the fact that there is more to ourselves than these thoughts and emotions that are churning out painful memories and self-doubts. If they could be alleviated in some degree, they might facilitate the movement of the steps. Some silence every day is a human need. Unless we have an opportunity for it on a regular basis, there is something missing in our lives. The human organism is refreshed and renewed by the experience of silence.

That is why you go out into nature and no matter who you are, even if you are an atheist, just looking at the beauties of nature or the mountains or the clouds is relaxing. It relaxes a mind that is constantly churning out thoughts and emotional reactions, which is exhausting, and increases the need for some kind of compensation such as alcohol.

TS: The people that go to that meditation meeting for the first time are impressed by the feelings of rest after that twenty minutes. But not only that, new depths of honesty and sharing seem to occur after sitting for twenty minutes in God's presence.

TK: Yes. It leads to the freedom to be more honest because one is being affirmed at a deep level, so that one no longer needs the old defenses or cover-up mechanisms. It is easier to be oneself, whoever that may be.

TS: St. Thérèse of Lisieux once wrote, "I think the smallest, most insignificant thing we do is supremely important in God's eyes if we do it in accordance with His will and out of love for God." I guess as alcoholics we should not forget that. Little accomplishments are important even in making amends.

TK: In her *Little Way*, as she calls her teaching, what is most important is love, not the difficulty of the action. Many small acts of love build up the courage to handle big acts of self-denial that may be required in going through the steps over and over again.

TS: Yes, sometimes we have to reassure our sponsees that they are doing the best they can. They may be doing a lot of small things, but in God's eyes these are beautiful actions, and He welcomes them just as He welcomes the major accomplishments.

TK: I venture to say that anyone who undertakes the Twelve Steps seriously is not just engaged in little deeds, but has taken on a very significant journey, which is of great value not only to them, but to their friends, their family, and all humanity.

Whenever you take up the spiritual journey in any form, and certainly the Twelve Steps is a form of spirituality, the whole human family goes with you. As you free yourself from the negativity that you pour into the atmosphere through the lack of respect for yourself and others, this positive energy helps the whole ecology of the universe.

There is a spiritual aspect to ecology. The evil of negativity that unredeemed people are pouring into the universe is balanced by the spiritual efforts of those who are sincerely trying to give themselves to God and do His will. The moment we turn to God, our whole past life means nothing to Him. He is only interested in the love that we now have, and that is manifested by taking up this practice and turning to God with sincerity. This is what repentance really means in the Christian tradition. Instead of looking for happiness in the wrong places, it means changing the direction where you are looking for happiness. The Twelve Steps is a path to finding out where it can be found.

TS: One final area: sometimes people we have harmed have passed on and we cannot make direct amends. What suggestions come to mind in making amends to people that have passed on?

TK: The first thought that immediately comes to mind is that we can pray for them and sometimes have others pray for them. Obviously, if you don't believe in a future life, that particular way of making amends might not appeal. Time is relative. Interior amends that are directed to somebody who has passed on may actually reach them, in virtue of the unity of the human family that transcends space and time.

In a sense we are all together in the present moment. This is the reality that is directly in front of us, and everything else is an interpretation of that reality. If we just sat down and asked people we offended in life for pardon, as if they were present, a deep reconciliation could take place.

This will at least have a good effect on us, but it also may have a great effect on them. This is not something that we can prove, but if you believe in the communion of saints, there is the interdependence of people who have died with those who are here and with those who are yet to come. If you have that kind of faith in the transcendent unity of the human family, then the prayers that we offer may really help them all. If you don't want to pray, just tell the people who have gone on that you are sorry. There is a lot of data in which people who have departed have made themselves felt to their loved ones, as if to say everything is okay with me. So it is possible and worthwhile to make amends even with those who have passed on

TS: A wonderful concept—thank you for that, Father. We can perhaps now move on to the tenth step.

STEP TEN

*Continued to take personal inventory and
when we were wrong, promptly admitted it.*

Tom S.: In step ten, Bill W. wrote that now "we can com-
mence to put our AA way of living to practical use, day by
day, in fair weather or foul." Bill also wrote "that no one
can make much of his life until self-searching becomes a
regular habit." Father, would you comment on what Bill
said about the importance of making self-searching a regular habit?

Thomas Keating: I know he recommended it once a day,
if I'm not mistaken. Maybe he was suggesting that it could
be even more often, so that whenever one notices that one is
having an experience of self-centeredness or selfishness, one
would notice it and immediately drop it.

    This is a rather advanced stage of the spiritual life in any
tradition. It means that one is ever mindful of one's immediate experience. One is sensitive to responding to the needs of
the present moment and also to the presence of God in every
passing nanosecond of time.

    There is a certain spiritual poise that forms as one walks
in the presence of God that enables one to perceive when
one's conduct is departing from what you have resolved

to do. This kind of sensitivity is called *living in the present moment*. God is only present in the present moment. There is no attachment to the past or future. Everything is present in this present moment. Our past life is only present insofar as it affects us in the present moment, so each moment is a way of relating to God with the whole of our being. This state requires a great capacity to be detached from our unconscious motivation that interferes with our intention, and keeps dragging us away from the present moment with thoughts about the past or plans for the future.

In other words, you would notice as soon as a little movement of vanity came in if you were doing a good deed. You would notice when you had some self-reflection that was negative or positive and instead of reflecting on it or encouraging the emotion, or trying to get away from the feeling of distress, you would simply acknowledge it and let it go.

TS: This sounds like a skill that has to be developed. Maybe it is in a rough stage the first time we do step ten, and then the skill develops as we get deeper and deeper into prayer and meditation.

TK: Exactly. To put it another way, I don't know how airplanes work today, but in an earlier period of aviation history they used to have an automatic pilot or they had a signal that would be a beep, and the pilot having ear phones on, if he was off course, would get one beep, to the right. If he was off course to the left, there would be two beeps, or some such system. When he was on dead center there would just be silence.

So, in the state that Bill W. is describing here in the tenth step, whenever you get off course, that is to say, whenever you forget the presence of God or whenever you get overly involved in some negative motivation, the beeper goes off. But when you are on course, that is, when your will is united to God, there is just peace without thinking about it. The beeps simply warn you when you are getting off course and are beginning to lose your peace. Then you adjust your course back by some little act of self-surrender to God such as, "My God I love you," or "I'm not doing this for me, but for you," or just "God," or put one's hand on one's breast. In other words, you renew your intention like you do in centering prayer, to consent to God's presence and action within you.

TS: I think those aspirations are important. They sometimes pop up in my consciousness without even thinking about it. That can be so reassuring. Perhaps we should be more cognizant of that when we are talking to our sponsees and offering different spiritual avenues to use. Is there a reference for aspirations that you could suggest?

TK: There are loads of them. You can also make up your own. It can be as short as you want, or a sentence you take from scripture such as, "Oh, God, come to my assistance," or "Not my will but thine be done."

TS: Perhaps the Psalms could be a resource.

TK: The scriptures are just loaded with them. You should choose one that you feel comfortable with or just make one up, inspired by the scripture.

TS: What a useful tool that is. Especially when we are facing something abnormal or threatening: to bring God's presence right to the floor. That is an excellent practice.

Bill mentioned there are three types of inventory. All are alike in principle. One is the spot-check inventory that we take any time of the day. The other is the occasional inventory, which we take maybe in the company of our sponsor or spiritual advisor. Then there is the occasional retreat—a day or so of "self-overhauling." Father, would you comment on the latter method, the retreat concept, and its benefits from your side of the aisle?

TK: Contemplative Outreach, the organization that supports those who have been instructed in centering prayer, provides different kinds of retreats, some are for a day, some a weekend, some ten days. There is one that is 21 days. So, obviously, the lengthier the time that you can profitably stay in silence and solitude, the more change you expose yourself to because the silence and solitude accompanied by centering prayer or some other non-conceptual form of prayer is cumulative in the deep rest that it brings to the psyche and consequently to the body because the two, body and soul, are so closely united that what one does the other always vibrates to. Whatever dance one is doing the other is the partner. You cannot avoid that. In that situation, one is always open to the movement of the Spirit and becomes more and more skilled, as Bill W. suggests. By *skill* I mean a habit of responding to God in every situation. A habit is something, by definition, that once it is established, is easy, delightful, and spontaneous.

A habit fulfills all of the aspects of what Bill W. is speaking. Habits can be acquired by our own efforts in some degree But the best habits and the most effective ones are those that are infused by the Holy Spirit. Once you are on the spiritual journey and established in grace, you have as part of your patrimony the seven-fold gifts of the Holy Spirit. Four of them are designed for active life and three for one's contemplative prayer periods. One of the active gifts is the gift of counsel in which the Spirit of God nudges us, not with words, but with attractions and inspirations, what to do in great detail in every moment of our lives, if we are willing. In other words, it is the Spirit that suggests the aspirations that you were talking about. It is the Spirit that suggests taking inventory. It is the Spirit that suggests it is time for you to take a retreat. You are perfectly free, but you have a sense that you are being led by a Higher Power and that the best thing you can do is follow that inspiration. It is the Spirit that enables us to do everything for the love of God. It is the Spirit that enables us to stay on course in that airplane I described, to experience peace during all of our activities, which is perhaps the greatest sign of God's presence at work in us.

The Spirit gets down to brass tacks and suggests when to get up, when to go to bed; what to eat, what not to eat; who to speak to, who not to speak to; what relationships to cultivate, and what not. Remember when Paul was going to go to one place in Greece, he had a vision saying, "Don't go there." Then he had a dream about somebody in Macedonia saying, "Come over and help us." So that is where he went.

We don't know the grand plan of God. We are just instruments. Joy consists in following with habitual submission the movements of the Spirit that rise up from deep within us and give us a certain conviction that we should do one thing rather than another.

If we can follow that inspiration without reflecting on it or thinking about it, it usually works out very well. A great deal of good can be accomplished without our thinking about it. At other times, the Spirit may urge us to do a lot of planning or thinking. The inspirations are very varied.

The Gift of Counsel is a treasure in daily life. It is like having someone over your shoulder that is your sponsor and spiritual director combined and vastly superior to both, because the Spirit knows everything that has happened, and he knows God's plan, and how well you can cooperate with God's plan. He would never ask you for too much. But he knows when to ask for more.

It is an incredible relationship that is opened up to us by the gifts of the Spirit once one is established in the grace of God.

TS: Getting established takes time. As a sponsor, I often find that you just have to keep encouraging the sponsee because it is developmental. And while the intuition may be in a rough stage in the beginning, eventually, if we follow the steps and the deep level suggested, especially the eleventh, I think we get to that point where we have fine-tuned our ability to listen to the Spirit and recognize what it is saying. Bill Wilson wrote about "justifiable anger." He said that it can lead to what he called emotional dry benders and then alcohol.

Father, would you comment on the passion of anger versus the energy of anger? There is something good about anger, as I understand it. But it is the passion of anger that gets us in trouble.

TK: We must not suppress the energy of anger, because it is basically the power in us that enables us to pursue the difficult good or persevere in tough situations. Anger is not designed to hit people over the head. It is not designed for revenge. These are the more primitive aspects of it, the passion. One can have anger without experiencing the passion of anger. One can have anger and deliberately stir up angry feelings in order to accomplish some good. Jesus evidently did when he threw the money changers out of the Temple.

He must have been furious, not just in an abstract sense. He scared them to death. They couldn't get out of there faster. It is sometimes appropriate to show anger. But the difference between passion and the energy of anger is that once the situation is ended, the passion continues and we find ourselves in a mood of anger. But the energy of anger stops when its purpose has been completed. So it leaves you ready for the next event with its proper emotional response, which might not be anger, but something else, such as joy, or love, or something like that. It is domination by the emotion of anger that is harmful, not the energy itself. That is a difficult distinction for people who are somewhat angry by temperament or by habit to recognize. I don't recommend presuming that one can exercise just anger too soon in the spiritual journey, because usually there turns out to be mixed motivation. Yes, we had a good intention, but we also had a strong wish to straighten this guy out or to get even, or put him in his place. All those attitudes are not the movement of the Spirit, but of the false self seeking compensation.

TS: I heard a fellow in AA say the other day, as far as fear is concerned, "Make friends with fear." He spoke about this sergeant in Korea. He always wanted to be with the soldiers that had fear, not the ones without fear, because the ones with fear were more alert and kept on looking around and took care of themselves. He said the fellows without fear could get you killed. It is an interesting observation.

I guess we could say that fear has a healthy side to it, too. Just like anger.

TK: Fear is always valuable in a dangerous situation. It creates the mechanism of fight or flight in the body, which is the path to survival in dangerous circumstances. But fear as a feeling is not productive. It is the opposite of love. Hence, Jesus says in the Gospel, "Fear is useless." By that he means the emotion of fear, not the fear that is associated with reverence and awe, which is not a passion, but a disposition of reverence and wonder. What fear means in the Bible most of the time does not mean the emotion of fear. That would not be a suitable disposition to have toward God whom we should trust. But what the fear of God means in scripture normally, according to some of the best exegetes, is to have the continuous loving awareness of God's presence.

TS: I'm glad you said that.

TK: Fear in scripture is not the feeling of fear, but the proper attitude to life. It is to be in the presence of reality all of the time.

TS: We hear so many sermons today where the speaker uses the term "fear of God," yet they never explain that it is not fear in the way we usually think of it. It is really trusting God or loving God.

TK: Yes, it is important for preachers and teachers to explain that to the young because we live in a psychological age in which fear is interpreted primarily as an emotion, not as reverence or awe.

A very misguided understanding of God could arise in the young, if the term is not explained as reverence and trust. Fear as an emotion is obviously not helpful to develop a relationship to God because no one wants to get any closer than necessary to something they fear.

TS: You once mentioned that primitive emotions are stored in the body. Could you comment on that?

TK: All repressed emotions are stored in the body. What I think you are referring to are the repressed emotions that we put into the unconscious, so as not feel them consciously. These are stored in the body as in a kind of warehouse, where they interfere with the free flow of grace and the natural energies of the body. To evacuate them is necessary for health. This is part of the work of divine therapy. The deep rest of contemplative prayer reduces the defenses that hold these oppressive feelings in the unconscious. They may come to awareness during centering prayer in the form of primitive thoughts such as panic, grief, discouragement, lust, or anger. We recommend that you disregard them because their negative or painful energy, once they reach your awareness, indicates that they are on the way out.

All you need to do is wave goodbye. It is just that if you hit a place where there is a lot of repressed material, this might go on for a few periods of prayer or a few days, or even last off and on for a significant number of days or weeks.

TS: If we don't do that, it is liable to affect our health and our immune system.

TK: It sure does. If it is anger, the tension closes the blood vessels. It hardens the arteries and could bring on a heart attack.

TS: I know fellows afflicted with AIDS. The ones that do better are the ones that approach that disease physically, mentally, and spiritually. Too many of them leave out the third part, the spiritual part, and concentrate on the physical.

Well, Father, if you don't have any further comments on step ten, we can just move into a couple of questions on step eleven.

STEP ELEVEN

Sought through prayer and meditation to improve our conscious contact with God as we understood Him, praying only for knowledge of His will for us and the power to carry that out.

Tom S.: Father Thomas, I have a few final questions on step eleven. Bill W. begins the eleventh step with this sentence: "Prayer and meditation are our principal means of conscious contact with God." We often hear different definitions of prayer versus meditation. I wonder, Father, if you would comment on what distinguishes one from the other?

Thomas Keating: Prayer is essentially a relationship with God. As soon as you say that, you introduce the idea of a process that grows from something that is fairly inchoate or awkward, to one that moves into friendliness or at-easeness in the relationship, then to a moment of commitment that we might call friendship. Friendship opens the door to other forms of union, which may lead to spiritual friendship or marriage.

In other words, various levels of union and communion become possible. We use vocal prayers or the prayers that the church offers us in the liturgy, because we don't know what else to say. We don't know where to begin. All we know is how to talk about the weather, and presumably God is not that interested in the weather, at least not as much as we are. But God is interested in us. What God listens to is not our words but our hearts, our inmost dispositions. This relationship can become more and more intimate and then it begins to use the more interior faculties of human nature, which are intuition and the spiritual will.

Meditation is a word that has had different meanings over the centuries. In Christian spiritual tradition, it usually means discursive meditation, the use of the imagination, intellect, and affective faculties.

When we are concentrating, we are directing our relationship from a place that is only a first step on the journey toward union and unity with God, levels that are much more satisfying and intimate.

In the Christian tradition, meditation usually means the use of the discursive intellect. It is thus a concentrative practice.

TS: In your writings, you use the term "contemplation" to differentiate between meditation in the Christian tradition and a deeper relationship with God. Could you give us a short definition of contemplation?

TK: By contemplation we mean communion, resting in the presence of God beyond feelings, particular acts of the will and concepts. That state we call *contemplation*. It is a movement from concentration to receptivity, from conversation to communion. It does not mean that we no longer converse with God at other times or in other forms of prayer, but we have a new capacity to be present with God and to commune with Him in silence.

TS: In AA sometimes you hear the comment, "Prayer is when we talk to God and meditation is when He talks to us." But I think that is an over-simplification because in meditation (or maybe a better term would be *contemplation*), I think God really talks to our heart, not to our intellect. And we know that He talks to the heart through the fruits of whatever we do. That sort of ties into your teaching on contemplation, that the individual usually doesn't sense the presence of God during the silent prayer, but through the fruits of meditation in daily life we know that God is present. Does that reflect what you said?

TK: I think I would rather say that God does not so much talk to us in contemplation as embrace us in contemplation. In other words, contemplative prayer is more like a kiss or a hug than a series of remarks. In a passionate kiss, the beloveds are expressing their desire to pour themselves into each other and to become united with each other, even to become the other.

Contemplation is the level of communion that moves into an intimacy that temporarily precludes conversation because of the nature of the union. When you are being kissed on the mouth, it is not the time to talk about the weather. The other person is only asking you to receive his or her love. Contemplation is an exchange of love for which all the other acts of conversation and service are sort of preliminaries.

At the same time, you do not spend your life in the bedroom. Intimacy has a significant role to play in the development of your relationship, but you have to bring back into everyday life the enhanced exchange of love in the way you serve the coffee in the morning and share the care of the children. It brings a level of deeper love into all of the other normal acts of shared life. The reciprocal action between movements of great love and everyday life is called the *spiritual marriage* in the Christian heritage, to emphasize the intimate experience of divine love that humans are capable of.

But it is only an analogy. The union is actually far more intimate than conjugal love.

In the Hebrew bible there is a wonderful poem, "The Song of Songs," which speaks of the union of God with the human soul in a way that is quite erotic. The Beloved expresses the most intense and passionate affection for the beauty and presence of the Beloved.

Meditation in the sense of thinking or talking is not appropriate for the level of intimacy that one deliberately exposes oneself to during the period of contemplative prayer. But then contemplative prayer manifests itself, as you said very well, in actions that manifest the tenderness and goodness of God in everyday life by showing love to others by practical concern and care for their needs.

The Eastern religions have come to the West and taught meditation in a different sense from the one usually given to it in the Christian tradition. In general, what they mean by meditation is what we mean by contemplation.

TS: Bill Wilson wrote that the purpose of prayer and medi-tation is "to improve our conscious contact with God." Since he wrote this, there has been so much written about the unconscious that I wonder if he would reword this step a little bit today and insert the concept of the unconscious. What are your thoughts on that?

TK: This is an interesting question. I would hesitate to speak for Bill W. He has others who can speak better than I on his behalf. I think all spiritual disciplines have to be reevaluated in regard to their explanation or articulation in the light of contemporary and ongoing discoveries in developmental and depth psychology and in other sciences that contribute to the understanding of reality such as anthropology, sociology, quan-tum mechanics, biophysics, and genetics, to mention a few. St. John of the Cross has a saying in which he says, "Human health consists in the conscious awareness of God." That is pretty close to what Bill W. is quoted as saying in this step. It is the unconscious presence of God becoming conscious that is the fruit of the spiritual journey and of the Twelve Steps as described in the twelfth. The whole purpose of the other steps is to become consciously aware of God's presence, which to us in the beginning is unconscious. I call it the *ontological uncon-scious*, which is the level of being, rather than the psychologi-cal unconscious, which refers to repressed emotional material in the unconscious. The collective unconscious is the shared experience of the human race that may also have significant influence on our conduct, attitudes, or belief systems.

The Divine Indwelling is a loving presence of God within us. It is unconscious to us in the beginning of the spiritual journey. As it becomes conscious, it gives us a signal as to where true happiness is to be found. When that happens, it reevaluates the importance that we gave to all of the other sources of happiness that we hoped or expected would bring us gratification. They are substitutes for God when we do not experience his presence.

Rooted in the Divine Indwelling, according to the Christian contemplative heritage, are the three theological virtues of faith, hope, and charity; the four infused moral virtues of temperance, fortitude, justice, prudence; the Fruits of the Holy Spirit of which there are nine according to St. Paul (Gal. 5): charity, joy, peace, gentleness, self-control, patience, goodness, generosity, and faithfulness; and finally the seven Gifts of the Holy Spirit.

As manifestations of our true self, these supernatural treasures are waiting to be activated or released in everyday life through the growing awareness of God's constant presence and the exercise of the Fruits of the Spirit: charity, joy, and peace. Charity is the unselfish love that seeks no reward, the kind of love that God has shown for us—the kind of love that enables us to forgive from the heart.

Joy enables us to avoid all discouragement. Peace, as St. Paul says, surpasses all understanding, or the ability to describe it to others.

Freud wrote about the reality of the unconscious. This is an energy that dwells in people as the result of repressed pain and trauma, which, unconscious to them, influence their ordinary behavior and even major decisions in life.

For instance, a typical one: someone marries another person because he wants to continue having the same capable mother to do the laundry or to dry his tears. Or one marries someone because she never had a father and this guy fits the bill. This is not going to be a happy marriage, because when the other person finds out that they were married for that reason, they want someone who is at least equal to them. So this marriage is in trouble unless the person recognizes the dynamic he is subjected to because of past experiences and tries to change it. If that does not happen, then the marriage is in trouble. People enter religious life for the same motive. If they were orphaned, they sometimes enter the community hoping to find the family they never had as children. This is not going to work unless they become aware of the problem and try to work to change it.

As the dark side of your personality comes to consciousness, then you have an opportunity to change your attitude and to be alert to negative movements. Otherwise one's relationships get fouled up. You can even enter a dysfunctional relationship with God and even try to manipulate Him.

TS: I know practice is so important. In AA, the practice is ecumenical. At my home group, we have maybe four or five different religions present at our weekly meditation meeting and we are all sitting in silence in God's presence.

TK: Silence is a great common denominator between people and also between us and God. God's first language is silence. Everything else is a poor translation. It is by entering into silence that we are best able to hear God.

St. John of the Cross expressed it in this way, "God the Father spoke only one word from all eternity. He spoke it in an eternal silence and it is only in silence that we hear it."

Meditation, in the contemplative sense, is making oneself vulnerable to the Ultimate Reality that we know loves us. This gives us the courage to face the dark side of our personality and gradually to process the undigested emotional material of a lifetime by allowing it to come to consciousness. We have to deal with our emotions including those we have repressed. We cannot just sit on them. But it does not require a lot of dealing. We just have to accept them, feel them, notice where they are in the body, and then give them to God to heal, or as a present.

TS: It sounds like, after all this discussion, the wording of the eleventh step is fine. We should just leave it the way it is.

TK: I would not change it. I would understand meditation in the sense of contemplative prayer, if you are a Christian. That is the only gloss I would offer.

TS: Father Thomas, how important is discipline in centering prayer or meditation?

TK: The main discipline is to sit down and shut up. And that is pretty difficult for most people. It doesn't just mean closing your mouth, however, but letting go of your usual stream of thoughts and the endless interior dialogue that goes on most of the day and night about what happens to us, or about people entering and leaving our lives.

TS: I found for myself that regardless of whether I felt like it or not, I had to put aside that time every day, and it is the constant repetition on a daily basis that helped me most.

TK: Our ordinary psychological awareness is opposed to silence, and nowadays many people have never experienced silence. So it takes a practice, a discipline, a routine, or constant repetition, similar to what you have to impose on the body when you are trying to learn some physical skill. This applies also to the mind. It has to be trained and disciplined. Repetition is one of the chief tools for creating new habits. Habits come from doing something the same way over and over again.

TS: Thanks, Father. I have just one remaining question on the eleventh step. How can a person who is non-religious but believes in a Higher Power beneficially use centering prayer to accomplish the meditation requirement of the eleventh step?

TK: Centering prayer has a very simple structure and the basic experience that it communicates, if it's done according to directions, is to awaken in us the realization of what silence is interiorly. In other words, it translates the experience of external quiet to the experience of being quiet inside. The imagination is a perpetual motion faculty, so it is usually grinding something out. To deliberately not talk to yourself for 20 minutes at a time undermines the thought patterns or structures that reinforce one's emotional programs for happiness. By not deliberately thinking *any* thought, you begin to undermine the habitual thought patterns of your whole life, which may be reinforcing the addiction you are suffering from. It is not hard to do and it does not require particular actions in daily life.

One begins to lose interest in the addictive process or in the addictions. Exposure to silence on a regular basis offers a kind of universal healing for everybody no matter what their religion—or if they are of no religion. It is an innate capacity of human nature. This silence is not dependent on having exterior silence (that's not always in our control), but of sitting with the deliberate intention to be in the presence of the Higher Power without judgment, reflection, plans, or memories. It is to be in the present moment with *That Which Is*, believing that we are loved just as we are.

Our consciousness is sustained at every moment by the greater consciousness that we call *God* in the Judeo-Christian tradition. But it's available to everybody because every human being has the capacity to be still. To quote one of the Psalms from the Hebrew scriptures, "Be still and know that I am God." This is not a rejection of mental activity as such, but a recognition of its limitations. Beyond our thoughts is the world of spirit that is characterized by realities that transcend our capacity to articulate them.

TS: Many thanks, Father. I think we have reached the end of the day here. Would you lead us out with a prayer?

TK: *Holy Spirit of God, we believe in Your presence within us. Anoint us with Your gifts, draw us inwardly to Your presence. Heal the wounds of our lifetimes and enable us to enter into the fullness of your divine presence, which is life, light, and Love without limit.*

STEP TWELVE

Having had a spiritual awakening as the result of these steps, we tried to carry this message to alcoholics and to practice these principles in all our affairs.

Tom S.: This afternoon we will review the last of the steps. The twelfth step is the longest in number of pages in *Twelve Steps and Twelve Traditions*. We do not have time today to cover all 19 pages of the twelfth step in which Bill Wilson summarizes the AA program and describes its full implication in the lives of its members. I have selected about 15 excerpts from the twelfth step, each a sentence or two, which I think capture the essence of this last step.

I'm going to read each excerpt and ask you, if you are interested, to comment on it or you may ask to move on to the next one if you feel that you've answered it already.

One of the first sentences that we come across in the twelfth step is this one: "Here we begin to practice all twelve steps of the program in our daily lives so that we and those about us may find emotional sobriety." Would you care to touch on that, or do you think we covered it already?

Thomas Keating: We touched on this before, but the idea

of emotional sobriety is so valuable, it might be worth coming back to it once more. It is obvious that this step refers to a transformation of consciousness that penetrates and encompasses the whole of our lives and all our relationships: God, other people, ourselves, the planet earth, and the cosmos.

Emotional sobriety is the same as detachment from our own ideas of happiness and also from our overdependency on the group to which we feel we belong, along with our cultural conditioning, education, personality traits, and emotional patterns.

In other words, all of these interior tendencies and outside influences added up to a false self based on our traumatic experiences from early life that we were trying to run away from all our lives, rather than face. Now through the Twelve Steps, you face them all, and as a result they have been relativized. The energy that we originally put in them, in our desperate search for happiness through emotional programs that couldn't possibly work, is now available for the service of God, other people, and to bring the message of AA to as many people as possible.

An enormous freedom has begun to be experienced, expressed in the ability to serve others, even heroically, with the view of helping them to climb out of the swamp of alcoholism or whatever the addiction is. We cannot do this without an ever deepening awareness of the motivation that lurks in our unconscious, since the unconscious energy is stored in the body and secretly influences our behavior and decisions.

We have to find out what this is in order to be able to let it go. Otherwise, it continues to insinuate itself into our decisions even the most important decisions in life, and we only find out afterward that there was something that was amiss in our motivation.

The sixth step of AA is crucial from this point of view because it says that we became *entirely* ready, not just ready. For me "entirely" includes the awareness of our unconscious motivation of just how askew our life's decision-making processes have been. We have been in a straitjacket of programs for happiness that haven't given us much room or flexibility to reach our own inner capacities as the image of God.

Here is the point I am trying to make. As we become aware of the dark side of our personality and how much energy we put into programs for security, power and affection, esteem and approval, we realize that we cannot manage our own lives. In other words, the first step has become an experience even deeper than the original one. Only now it is not a desperate state of mind, but self-knowledge that has grown to include parts of our personality that we didn't know because often we had projected the dark side of our personality onto someone else. Now we are confronted with who we actually are with all our brokenness and our weakness. Once we have turned our life over to God, we have the capacity to endure that humiliating recognition that we can't do anything to take away our faults. Then we're entirely ready to have them taken away.

We don't even start praying yet to take them away

because we know that secretly we like some of them. And so we plead with God to take them away. Our willingness that He do so is the best prayer of all. We don't have to put it in words. If we do, "Help me," says it all. And then God takes them away. The healing is not something you and I do, whether it's in the AA or in the Christian traditions. It's something that God does in us with our permission. In addition to that, we put up so many obstacles that God has a hard time doing what He wants in us. God respects our freedom and waits until we are entirely ready for Him to take away our faults. The sixth step summarizes everything that went before in the way of self-knowledge and emphasizes not only the dark side that we experienced in the first step, but also the growing confidence in God that is the result of turning our life over completely to the Higher Power.

TS: Let's move on to the next excerpt. That reads: "As a result of practicing all the steps, we have each found something called a spiritual awakening." Would you like to touch on what you've called the *mysterium*—what did you call it?

TK: *Mysterium tremendum et fascinans*. Such an experience certainly brings about an awakening. Sometimes it involves a sudden breakthrough, but more often it's gradual, more of a process. The true self is awakening as the false self goes to sleep.

TS: It dies?

TK: At least its intensity is reduced. We never completely lose our temperamental traits. But it's hard to often distinguish them in people with a certain integration and authenticity, which makes them effective in every service or ministry that they may engage in.

TS: The next excerpt reads: "He has been granted a gift which amounts to a new state of consciousness and being."

TK: A self-awakening is an expanded state of consciousness that doesn't limit our relationship to God to rational reflections on the divine attributes. These, at most, are just pointers toward the Mystery. The self-awakened person is tasting something of the Mystery itself without the intermediary of thoughts. This experience is vastly more intimate. It brings us to embrace the Divine Goodness, presence, and love. It translates into seeing all of life with its events, its tragedies, its disasters, the past and the future, in terms of a much broader plan than just one generation, so that it's naturally a humbling experience. As St. Teresa of Avila wrote, the greatest source of humility is not thinking how bad you are. It's rather the direct experience of God, which is humbling of its very nature. That's what *mysterium tremendum* is all about. One sees one's nothingness and that without God we're nothing. We also realize that we are not an object, no particular thing, and hence we can relate to reality in an expanded kind of consciousness. We are able to perceive reality from God's point of view. Even deep personal tragedy is not just tragedy, but rather an invitation to new depths of self-knowledge, understanding, and service of others. Suffering in this viewpoint is a participation in the redemption of the human family.

TS: Bill Wilson relates to your comments in the next excerpt from step twelve—"The persistent use of meditation and prayer, we found, did open the channel so that where there had been a trickle, there was now a river, which led to sure power and safe guidance from God."

He writes about the persistent use, not just the occasional. I think one of the keys to emotional sobriety is persistence or some type of discipline in meditation and prayer.

TK: This ideal of fidelity to the steps and to working them every day, and working them into one's life, corresponds closely to what St. Paul calls *unceasing prayer*, which corresponds to the gift of the Holy Spirit called *reverence*, the capacity to be continuously in the presence of God. Obviously, we have to strive in daily life to remember God's presence. But after the awakening pointed to in the twelfth step, you don't have so much trouble in remembering God. In fact, it's well nigh impossible to forget Him. St. John of the Cross says, "Human health consists in the continuous and conscious experience of God's presence." It won't make you live in this world forever, but it certainly will reduce a lot of symptoms.

TS: And bring you to the "joy of living" level.

TK: Exactly, now you're open to joy. The afflictions of old age or illness are trivial compared to your interior enlightenment. You mentioned water as a symbol. Christ said, "One who believes in me, out of his inmost being will flow rivers of living water." So there's a lot of resources there, you just haven't discovered this artesian well that flows within us yet. After you've been enlightened according to the eleventh step, this water flows and nourishes all the other faculties, including our bodies. We can think straight, serve others, love people, forgive our enemies, find God everywhere, see all things in God. All kinds of treasures keep tumbling out of this totally spontaneous resource that was always there, but covered over and squashed by the false self and the development of the ego.

TS: Here's an excerpt that you touched on already, but I'll read it: "Can we accept poverty, sickness, loneliness and bereavement with courage and serenity?"... "Can we transform these calamities into assets, sources of growth, and comfort to ourselves and those about us? We surely have a chance ... if we are willing to receive that grace from God that can sustain and strengthen us in any catastrophe."

TK: This is strong teaching, but very solid, accurate, and true. This is precisely what I would call *emotional stability*. Even when you're blasted by personal tragedy or humiliation, as soon as you accept it, as this process enables you to do more and more easily, the water starts to flow. And even though the situation may be very painful, the pain doesn't blow you away, nor does it cause discouragement. You can transform the pain into joy because you are enduring it for the love of God. Faith perceives the situation as an opportunity to surrender even more completely to the divine action. It is a movement into a deeper communion with the will of God, which is obviously more difficult when things are rough.

TS: Bill writes about spiritual development in the next excerpt. "Only by this means can we improve our chances for really happy and useful living. As we grow spiritually, we find that our attitudes toward our instincts need to undergo drastic revisions."

TK: This is exactly what I mean by getting acquainted with the unconscious where the instincts are prominent. Our unconscious consists of all of the things that were too painful to bear for us as infants, because of our desperate need for security symbols, affection symbols, and control symbols. The residue of pain that has never been faced resonates with rejections in adult life. The present trial itself may not be earth-shattering, but the feeling of rejection may be intense not because the situation is that bad, but because it reminds us of an earlier experience where as a child we felt raw rejection.

In centering prayer, one of its primary therapeutic effects is that it enables deeply hidden primitive emotions to pass through our awareness during prayer without resisting or hanging onto them, judging them, or judging ourselves. It is a great service to ourselves and our relationships to face that kind of pain. To want to face the dark side of our personality and to want God to show us the truth about ourselves, takes a lot of motivation.

TS: Bill writes: "When we developed still more, we discovered the best possible source of emotional stability to be God Himself." Would you like to comment on that? Quite an insight on the part of Bill.

TK: This is what the process of divine intimacy is all about, discovering who God is. Not through reason or reflection, but through the experience of ourselves as a mirror of God's presence. At that level, knowing God and knowing self become the same thing. So it's a question of developing, as Bill W. says, our capacity to perceive this. Security doesn't consist in more houses, more cars, more insurance, as desirable as that might be. They'll fail us or drop away. When we die, they're not going to accompany us like the chariots in the pharaohs' tombs. God is the true security. Everything else is marginal. True freedom is union with God's will. True power is to draw on the divine empowerment. Finally, "God is love," as John says. Our heart's longing for happiness can only find complete rest in God.

TS: The next three excerpts I'll combine into one. In one sentence, Bill says: "We were still the victims of unreasonable fears." The next one is: "False pride became the reverse side of that ruinous coin called Fear." And the third excerpt is: "At heart, we had all been abnormally fearful."

TK: Do you know what he thought we were fearful of?

TS: I think he was referring to emotional feelings that are expressed through abnormal anxieties or fears that the non-alcoholic usually doesn't have to cope with. Part of the problem is that for years alcohol helped us to avoid these feelings and relieved us of the realities of life. When we stopped drinking, all that stuff started coming up, the reality of what happened, the way we lived, what we have been doing, and this experience becomes almost unbearable.

TK: Jesus says in the Gospels that fear is useless. And he often challenges the disciples about what they're afraid of. Fear as an emotion sets off the fight or flight reaction. If the fight or flight is going off all the time, our poor body and bloodstream is being filled with hormones such as cortisone and adrenaline. When this is repeated constantly, the body has an abnormal amount of these hormones flowing through it. If anxiety is pervasive, naturally the amount of fear is going to be abnormal and, hence, calls for extreme remedies or remedies that are close to hand or that worked before; and these can be dangerous for our health, not to mention the other disadvantages of being under the influence that distress our relatives and friends.

In centering prayer, we have a saying, "No thought is worth thinking about." It comes from one of our early spiritual guides, Mary Mrozowski. One of the things that is very helpful in the process of healing the unconscious is to see that we are not identified with our thoughts or our feelings, or our bodies for that matter. We have bodies. We have feelings and we have thoughts, but if you know you're not them, and don't identify with them, you can change them. This insight relativizes the domination that they have over most people who have not yet begun the healing process of self-knowledge. This term in the Christian tradition is basically the exposure to the contents of our unconscious as a result of deep rest and trust in God and what we call contemplative prayer.

TS: Here's an interesting comment Bill makes. He says: "A number of eminent psychologists and doctors made an exhaustive study. These distinguished gentlemen had the nerve to say that most of the alcoholics under investigation were still childish, emotionally sensitive, and grandiose."

TK: It also applies to people who have any addiction or who are under the influence of the addictive process and just haven't focused on a particular addiction yet.

TS: Bill also writes: "True ambition is the deep desire to live usefully and walk humbly under the grace of God."

TK: I have no argument with that. It sort of resonates with one of the great Jewish prophets of Israel, who said, "We should do what is right and walk humbly before God."

TS: In our last excerpt, Bill writes: "Understanding is the key to right principles and attitudes. Right action is the key to good living."

TK: He has articulated very well the fundamental bases of all virtue in that twelfth step commentary.

TS: We have covered the essence here, I hope, and maybe we can move on to a few closing questions.

Father Ed Dowling was a Jesuit and, as noted, a very good friend of Bill Wilson. Bill referred to him as "the greatest and most gentle soul I may ever know." He wrote a letter to Bill, I guess it was in the middle 1950s, and he mentioned in the letter: "If AA spent less time and energy in the breadth dimension of spreading AA and more in the length and depth dimension, the breadth of the spread may not be limited to such a low percentage of the world's alcoholics."

In other words, he's saying by deepening the lives of AA members, presumably through prayer and meditation, he felt that AA would attract a higher percentage of the world's alcoholics. I don't mean for you to become critical of AA, Father Thomas, but I would like to hear your thoughts regarding Father Ed's comments.

TK: This is a way of suggesting that centering prayer, which has all of those objectives as a part of its program, might be something worth introducing in the Twelve Step program. At least at the eleventh, but possibly a little earlier, such as at the sixth.

TS: I agree. My sense is, as members meditate more on a regular basis and grow into deeper spiritual levels, they begin to reflect the principles of AA in such a way that it becomes obvious in their discussions with others or at meetings. It just emanates, and that may be what Father Dowling is talking about.

TK: The people you are describing embody the wisdom of the Twelve Steps traditions and hence their witness, even regardless of what they say, is projecting a message of hope and reassurance that these steps really work. I would agree very much with Father Dowling on this point. I think the same principle applies to any form of spirituality. It's not in converting more people, but enabling those who have connected with it to go on developing deeper and deeper levels of penetration into the Mystery. This is what awakening means. It's not a privatized journey but immediately overflows on everybody else in one's environment, and probably on the human family as a whole. It has been said, by I think some cutting-edge medical person, that you cannot have a thought without affecting the whole universe instantaneously. If this happens with any thought, how much more will a thought that is emerging from someone who has negotiated these steps and has reached an awakened state of mind benefit many others. Such a person is pouring positive energy and divine life and light and love into the universe, but especially into the atmosphere of our planet that is, at present, an abyss of human misery collected over centuries from the violence and brutality of humans that are afflicted by the false self, and societies made up of false selves that have tried to solve problems by violence and domination, rather than by the human way of functioning through dialogue, negotiation, collaboration, compassion, and harmony.

TS: I have an interesting question for you. How can one test oneself to determine if one has done the steps in depth?

TK: I don't know the answer to that because I haven't formally done the steps. So maybe that's a question you should answer.

TS: Well, I would say, "How do you test when an alcoholic has rejoined the human race?" It's a difficult question.

TK: Maybe you don't really have to know. Just keep trying.

TS: I suspect it is through the eyes of others. As an alcoholic does the steps in depth, often he cannot see his own growth. Just in conversing with his own sponsor or other people outside AA, or inside AA, he begins to see who he is in a different dimension from where he was, and it is very rewarding, although sometimes society doesn't appreciate the individual that is in front of them. They see him still in the old way and the alcoholic has to somehow gird himself up and say, "I'm a different person. They may not think I'm a different person, but I am," and I guess some faith is involved there.

TK: And courage.

TS: I think the key is, for the alcoholic, to say, "It's more important what God thinks of me than what everybody else thinks of me."

TK: Yes.

TS: And when you reach that point and really believe that, maybe you have gotten the steps in depth.

TK: That might be a very good criterion.

TS: The next question sort of ties into what we just said. In the *Heart of the World*, you wrote that, for traditional teachings to become part of us, they "must pass through our minds and hearts and become our own and emerge in our lives as a revelation of our [true self] here and now." I suppose we could say—if we really want to absorb the steps in depth— the traditional teachings of AA must pass through our minds and hearts and become our own, and emerge in our lives as a revelation of our true selves here and now.

TK: That's the purpose of the two aspects of practices of the Christian contemplative tradition that we talked about in the first lecture. So here are two practices, two how-to methods that we offer. They represent the experience of many generations and have their counterparts in almost all the world religions, as far as I can see. I think AA has to accept its mission as a spirituality, not only for alcoholics, but for our time, since it addresses, head-on, the human condition across the board, which may have extreme consequences in the case of alcoholics, but also is very damaging in other forms of addiction and for people who are under the influence of the addictive process.

TS: That touches on the next question. Bruce Shear, the founder of Pioneer Behavioral Healthcare, estimates that 23 percent of American adults and 20 percent of children suffer from mental disorders in a given year, mostly stress related.

Father Dowling wrote an article in the early days of AA headed: "AA steps for the Underprivileged, non-AA." Father Dowling was not an alcoholic, but he always felt that the AA steps could be quite useful to the "underprivileged non-AA" population.

Father Keating, do you see any way that our work and discussions today could reach non-alcoholics and perhaps bring them to the same spiritual healing levels that we have encountered in the Twelve Steps?

TK: I certainly think so and in the conceptual background of centering prayer, most of these principles appear, both in the unloading of the unconscious as well as the trans-formation of consciousness. All of these things are part of a program that emerges from the Christian contemplative tradition, and are described in different ways by different spiritual teachers throughout the centuries, but they amount to pretty much the same thing. What Bill W. and company have done, I don't know if they're aware of it, is to summa-rize the essence of the Christian contemplative tradition and put it in a form that is relatively simple, straightforward, and clear. Since everybody participates in the human condition, since they live in this world, everybody can benefit from the achievement of the Twelve Steps if they want to. So it really is a program that, it seems to me, anyone interested in spiri-tual development could do with great benefit to themselves, no matter what their religious form of expression is. And if you study the advice or the spiritual wisdom of the different traditions, you'll see that they all have insight into the same basic principles, maybe a little more emphasis on this or that step. The first five or six steps were largely inspired by the Oxford Group, which was a renewal of Christian spirituality in the Anglican community in the early part of the nineteenth century. Bill W. moved beyond them and created the other steps. But in doing so, he also seemed to remain in some contact with the Christian traditions through Father Dowling, and perhaps others. What Bill W. has done is to present a succinct and thorough expression of the Christian contemplative traditions in a nonsectarian form available to everyone. The reason not everyone benefits from it is because they would not do the steps. They would not take the means to develop their faculties so that they can face the dark side of the unconscious and allow the divine action to heal them, and in doing so, completely activate the innate powers of the soul or spirit to fly free. A symbol of a tradition often used is the transformation of a caterpillar into a butterfly. The two inhabit different worlds. And it really is that difference, from the life we had when we were in the straitjacket of the false self. It is a whole other world. You are not out of this world but you are no longer in it in the sense of being attached to it. It is there and that is where your service works itself out. And so I think the Twelve Steps could be used more by people pursuing the spiritual journey. All of the practical points of the steps would make for a very good spiritual practice for nonaddicted persons. You would use the steps of AA to bring the effects of centering prayer into everyday life.

TS: Thank you, Father. This concludes our interview on the twelfth step.

We are grateful for the generous commitment of your time and energy in making these interviews possible. May God bless you always.

PART II

Doing the Steps in Depth

DOING THE STEPS
IN DEPTH

In 1958 Bill W. wrote that many AA oldsters still find that they often lack "emotional sobriety." (See Appendix A for Bill's article.) There is much evidence that this problem still exists. Bill also wrote that this level of healing cannot be attained "until our paralyzing dependencies are broken and broken in depth." In reflecting on Bill's words, I kept coming back to the words "in depth." Was that the ingredient left out by these "oldsters"? Did they skate through the steps? Did they miss making what I call the twelve-inch trip from the intellect to the heart?

I think we all share one natural inclination—we don't like change. We set up mental roadblocks to change. God can remove these roadblocks. But He requires our consent. In AA we admit this in the sixth and seventh steps. I think Bill W. would agree that the depth of our sobriety is directly related to the openness with which we receive and live the words expressed in *Twelve Steps and Twelve Traditions*.

Which brings me to the purpose of Part II. Since the early days, monks have used a special prayer practice to cultivate their ability to absorb the Word of God (scripture) at deep levels and intuitively live the life that God had intended for them. In the eleventh century, this practice was given the Latin label "Lectio Divina," which means reading or, more exactly, "listening to scripture," as if God were speaking to the reader individually. What a gift it would be if we were able to develop a similar practice for AA members to help them in their quest to intuitively live the Twelve Steps.

In the following interview with Father Thomas, we touch on the possibility that the Twelve Steps are divinely inspired. We will also discuss the possibility of converting the ancient practice of Lectio Divina into a nonsectarian process that would be acceptable in AA circles.

Anyone can use this simple method for absorbing the words of an inspired book. I believe if a member of the Twelve Step community adopts any portion of what Father Thomas suggests, it will bring him or her a step closer to the doorway of a new "spiritual awakening."

—Tom S.

THE INTERVIEW

Tom S.: My name is Tom S. and I am an alcoholic.

Father Thomas, would you start us off today by commenting on the spiritual nature of the Twelve Steps?

Thomas Keating: I'd be glad to try. Most spiritual traditions have a wisdom literature. Alcoholics Anonymous, it seems to me, is a spiritual tradition. Its influence and spread in the present century is going to depend a lot on how well each generation of those in recovery assimilate and interiorize the basic wisdom that is enshrined in the Twelve Steps and the Twelve Traditions.

There is nothing new about reading an inspired text in a special way—with a certain discipline and reverence—that prepares the faculties—body, soul, and spirit—to access the goal of every spiritual practice, which is intimacy with the Divine. I realize that for beginners in AA, the group itself may be regarded as the Higher Power—or even something else.

In the great spiritual traditions of the world, there are many sacred texts like the Vedas and Upanishads in Hinduism, the Buddhist Sutras, the Qu'ran in Islam, the Hebrew bible, and the New Testament—just to mention a few.

TS: You mentioned "intimacy with the Higher Power." Can that be attained through the Twelve Steps?

TK: What you seem to be asking me to do is to review the basic ingredients of how to read the inspired texts of AA in a way that furthers accessing the spiritual dimension of the Higher Power and which points to where true happiness is to be found.

In other words, reading an inspired text in a special way is a highly tested and broadly experienced procedure for interiorizing the wisdom of a particular tradition. We are talking about the Twelve Steps of AA, which if it is not a sacred text at least is a very important text. After all, it presents people with the choice of life or death. So we better listen carefully to it.

The process of accessing divine intimacy presupposes how to read the texts of AA in such a way that our human faculties—body, soul, and spirit—are prepared to receive the gift of wisdom that the authors and the community of AA are trying to pass on.

TS: In the past, you have referred to "Higher Power" as *Mystery*. Could you comment on that?

TK: Here, Mystery is not in the sense of some novel or drama, but in the sense of a truth, experience, or presence that is beyond our reach at this point in our life, but at times kind of intuited, if it is only through the sense of desperate need. To feel one's life unmanageable is itself an experience of the divine.

Who says our life is unmanageable? Something deep within us—our personal experience—the disarray of our relationships, business, ministry, or with our family. All of these things point to a Presence that is challenging us—sometimes accusing us of missing the mark and losing what we had hoped would provide us with happiness. The happiness is there. The deepest root of our being is—at least in the Christian tradition—the image of God. This is reflected in the Buddhist tradition of Buddha Nature or in the Hindu tradition of the Atman. The Atman is a spark of the divine that dwells in each of us. The Hebrew bible and New Testament call it the image of God in us. More precisely, God, which is the term for the Ultimate Reality in the Judeo-Christian tradition, has created us in His own image. That is to say, the goodness, tenderness, beauty, and love of God is mirrored in us at the deepest level of our being. It is in accessing the root and source of our being that we find out what true happiness is, not in seeking it in things that cannot satisfy and in self-made programs for happiness that simply do not work. The ensuing emotional frustrations have brought many people to the first stage of AA, in which they realize profoundly and existentially that none of their programs for happiness are working for them or ever will work.

Let us look at this process of accessing the True Self—the image of God within us—or the Higher Power. The Buddhists call it Buddha Nature. The Zen tradition calls it the Absolute Self—capital "S" as opposed to the false self with a small "s," our day-to-day psychological experience of ourselves. The false self is basically an illusion. It is the epitome of what we mean by the human condition experienced without the presence of what true happiness is or any idea of where to find it.

TS: In regard to accessing the true self, I have prepared a chart below that, in very brief form, summarizes the four-stage process that monks have used for centuries to access, absorb, and live their sacred texts. How can we, in AA, adopt these steps in our quest for divine intimacy or a spiritual awakening?

The Process of Divine Intimacy			
Reading as Listening to God	Reflecting Ruminating Pondering	Responding Spontaneous Prayer	Resting in God's Presence

TK: The first step in reading a sacred text is to reverence it. Listen to it with receptivity, respect and welcome it. I know that you read a few pages from *Twelve Steps and Twelve Traditions* as part of your AA ritual. Sacred objects and texts usually have a certain ritual built around them. It is human nature to symbolize the significant experiences that one is perceiving or receiving. For example, every time you gather in an AA group meeting, someone says, "I'm Butch, and I'm an alcoholic"—you identify yourself. Then you have a special reading, and from there you launch out into the experience of the meeting, following certain rules and procedures, and finally you end with the Serenity Prayer or something similar. I haven't attended enough AA meetings to have memorized the ritual. But there is obviously an attempt to impress upon those who come that this is a very special meeting. Hence, the participants have to be present with all their faculties and attentiveness. This attentiveness is important when the text is read in public. The text needs to be proclaimed, not just read. Not just anybody should pick up the book and read, but only someone who has had the time to read the text beforehand and reflected on it, and who can articulate the words clearly so that everyone in the room can hear them. The reader should be able to give a certain emphasis to important sentences and words without putting oneself on display so to speak.

TS: Since being attentive is so important, would you suggest a prayer to start the meeting?

TK: Just coming together to relate to one's Higher Power is itself prayer. We tend to narrow the term "prayer" to particular words. Prayer primarily means relationship with the Higher Power. In the language of the Abrahamic religions, it is one's relationship with God. What I'm going to present as the process of divine intimacy is a path to assimilating and being assimilated by what for AA people is their inspired text—whatever they mean by *inspired*. The text is significant. It is life changing. It is a choice between life and death—at least for many people.

Suppose then that this text is read in public and everyone listens in silent, respectful attentiveness, and receptivity. It must be presented so that the meaning can be grasped by everybody. As the text is read again and again, people will begin to see certain aspects that they did not see in the beginning. Each time it is repeated there is the possibility of new insights from particular words or phrases, or in the reading as a whole.

TS: You have used the term "reading in public." Is this an umbrella term for any reading that is not private? And does it include reading at an AA meeting?

TK: Yes. It would also include reading at an AA Twelve Step meeting.

TS: Often at regular step meetings we read the full text of the step (each person reads a paragraph) and then we share our individual experiences regarding the step. Such meetings have been very effective and I have attended over 2,000 step meetings over the past 30 years. Our discussion today seems to be centering on a new option for individuals seeking a deeper absorption of the steps. With your permission, we can probably call this option a "Contemplative Step meeting."

I assume that such a meeting should be structured so that the various stages in the process of divine intimacy (see chart on p. 182) would be experienced by the attending members. What suggestions would you offer regarding the format for a Contemplative Step meeting?

TK: To benefit from a Contemplative Step meeting, the group does not have to journey through the whole fourfold process every time. Just the slow prayerful reading of one paragraph can be very rewarding. It may be enough to fill a period of silence after the text has been proclaimed to stimulate more useful and inspiring reflections. The period of silence after the reading might be three or four minutes for silent reflection.

If there is time, read the same section again and suggest to those present to respond inwardly to the thoughts that arose by asking the Higher Power to establish similar dispositions within them. If an attraction for interior silence or peace arises, invite everyone to relax into it without thinking. When this final experience does not arise, continue to respond in one's own words to the thought or thoughts that arose spontaneously after the first reading. The whole process can be completed in 10 or 15 minutes, expanding or limiting the two periods of silence as may work out best for the group.

A final step could be added from time to time (e.g., once or twice a week or month). Read the passage a third time and have the leader invite the group to share briefly their experience of interior peace or their insights that arose from the reading with the group.

TS: It seems to me that a sponsor could profitably convert the group format to a one-on-one format when covering a particular step (in depth) with a new sponsee. Do you agree?

TK: Absolutely.

TS: Does reading in private by yourself also involve four stages?

TK: To assimilate sacred texts, reading in private is just as important and often more important than reading in public. I mention the public aspect of it because it is already part of the ritual of the meeting. To get the full benefit of a sacred text, you need to be in the situation where somebody else is reading the text and you are just listening.

In this process of divine intimacy, when you are reading the text in private, you can stop at any time in order to reflect and respond in the presence of the Higher Power to the insights that you may be receiving. You do not have to read the whole text through to benefit from the process. As time goes on, you may only need to read one sentence to be completely absorbed in some insight or emotion that the text has given rise to.

Since this kind of reading is a very significant aspect of daily life, it needs a vestibule—a sort of remote preparation before you begin. You may also find it helpful to choose a place that is quiet where you won't be interrupted, and where you can prolong your concentration. You may also wish to fix a certain minimal time in which to do this. Perhaps twenty minutes or half-an-hour might not be too long, but certainly at least fifteen minutes to get into the text is recommended. When you have more leisure, you might add more. In other words, this method is a method-less procedure. You can do what you feel attracted to do within the parameters of reading, reflecting, responding to what you reflect on, culminating in moments in which you rest in the thought or insight or emotional effect that you might be experiencing.

Sacred reading that we do in private will go better if before we sit down we have somewhat dissipated our preoccupations and any form of tension. This calming procedure can be done in a number of ways, such as light physical exercises, walking around the block, having a cup of tea, or reading something that releases us from the preoccupations that we might be having. In this way when we sit down, we are not sitting down on red-hot coals or a stick of dynamite. When we sit down, the body can then be and remain in repose and quiet. Besides preparing the body, our imagination and memory need to be focused by a brief prayer or reading that is short—maybe half-a-minute or more, depending on how upset you are.

This approach is based on the four aspects of the traditional practice of Lectio Divina in the Christian tradition, which means reading what we believe to be divinely inspired texts. Thousands of monks from the third and fourth centuries on have used this process leading to divine intimacy. As the central focus of their training, it could be looked upon as a kind of distillation of the essence of their relationship with the Higher Power.

TS: How does the monastic reading tradition differ from ordinary reading?

TK: The experience of sacred reading is not like other kinds of reading. It is not even like reading a spiritual book. It is about listening to God who is believed to be the inspirer of particular texts. Even when you are doing it privately, you are not just reading; you are *listening*. The monks even said the words out loud when they read privately in order to impress the text on their bodies as well as on their minds. The two are closely interrelated.

The principles on which the monastic relationship with the Higher Power are based are silence, solitude, a discipline of prayer, and simplicity of lifestyle. To really read or hear a sacred text, it is also helpful to simplify daily life in regard to over-eating, over-entertainment, and over-work. In other words, to balance body, soul, and spirit so that each part of us receives nourishment from the spiritual source on a regular basis. It is like spiritual food and normal food—you need both every day.

Having settled down in this vestibule, we enter the actual listening process. Normally we will want to read the text through several times, but at some point we need to be alerted to the fact that God is speaking to us through this text. And to listen involves letting go of all the noise around us and within us and our preoccupations and concerns about anything at all.

Just think for a moment about what the process of listening to anything involves. What are you doing when you are listening deeply to something like music or a gifted speaker? Nothing at all! The less you do—body, mind, and spirit—and the more you simply attend to what is being said or heard, the more satisfaction, enrichment, and nourishment you actually receive from the beauty of the music or the insights. Listening is the opposite of being uptight; it is being fully attentive to the text and nothing else. Thoughts that arise that are extraneous are simply ignored. That is why the significance of the text needs to be a high priority when we sit down in the first place. This is the time to give oneself to the listening process and nothing else.

One reads not to dominate the text, but to receive the text, to assimilate it, and to be assimilated by it. This is a totally different process from the casual reading of a newspaper or a novel that is interesting or exciting—both of which have their value, but not in this kind of reading.

To repeat, it doesn't matter how much of the text you actually read.

TS: At what point do you suggest we pause in our reading or listen to the text and begin the second stage of the process: *Reflecting*?

TK: You read until some passage strikes you or moves you to reflect with your own thoughts on what the author has said. This is an invitation to put down the particular text you're reading and allow your imagination, memory, and conceptual apparatus to operate. It may involve reflecting on certain aspects of your life, memories, or the life situations that you are in. But you don't have to decide anything. You are just listening and using your mind to cultivate the insights you are receiving and to develop them in your own way. When a particular insight subsides, you may continue to read on. In this way you sort of weave your way through the text. The warp and woof of the process is your intention to listen and your practical attentiveness manifested by not pursuing other thoughts that intervene from whatever source, such as sense perceptions, memories, or plans for the future.

TS: I detect that the movement between the stages of divine intimacy is intuitive. What happens toward the end of the *reflecting* stage that signals a move to a *spontaneous* stage?

TK: When thoughts or insights are especially powerful, there is a kind of "aha" experience. Something you read strikes your intuitive apparatus and you say, "That's me," or, "I know what that means," or, "I've experienced that." When your emotions and feelings begin to be involved, this vastly improves your concentration on the text. Now you are in relationship with something or someone. You could call it your Higher Power. Actually, you are in relationship with the greatest teacher there is. You're in relationship with a personal love that is overwhelming and incomprehensible, but none the less real, and which manifests itself not directly but through the peace, encouragement, or instruction you are receiving.

These dispositions are signs that someone is enriching you in this encounter, which is almost like a conversation. In a sense, it is a conversation in which the text that you are reading provides the topic for discussion. So, out of a sense of reverence for this great teacher that the Higher Power is, one does not follow one's own thoughts all over the place, but tries to maintain a respectful attentiveness by keeping to the topics of conversation that are engaging one's mind and may be beginning to speak to one's heart.

Notice the progression here. First, reading as listening, even to the point of saying the words out loud—reading with attentiveness, respect, and receptivity. These dispositions may unfold into a kind of invitation to reflect on some particular part of the text such as a sentence or even just one word. You may read the same passage several times in order to fix it in your mind and to make sure that you mine all the riches that are contained in it. When the attraction subsides, you go back to the text and read a little more. You have the greatest flexibility to follow your inner attraction either just to read, listen, or reflect. Once your emotions and feelings are involved, you can express them inwardly through varied petitions or acts of gratitude, praise, and love—all of these dispositions may arise spontaneously. Sometimes there may arise a sense of being united to something (or someone): you don't know what or whom—but you know that it is extremely refreshing, nurturing, and loving.

TS: This sounds like a pathway to true peace of mind. How would you describe the healing that occurs at the instinctual level using this process?

TK: This positive experience begins to heal the deep wounds of self-hatred that may have arisen from the collapse of our expectations for happiness coming from our false self and the lack of esteem we have for ourselves because of having failed to meet the ideals of perfection or worldly success that we formerly envisaged. By worldly success, I mean material, professional, social, and all other forms of success that the world holds out as great sources of satisfaction. The whole cultural attitude toward success is relativized in this experience of finding out or perceiving the hollowness of the consumerist or materialistic objectives that advertising, the popular culture, and the mass media tend to pour into our consciousness twenty-four hours a day. The constant propaganda contrary to the values of a sacred text and its practical consequences for us requires the repetition of the same basic principles or values over and over again. Otherwise they will be drowned out by the pressures coming from outside. Then the habits of listening, not to the sacred text but to the promises of the advertisers, which always appeal to one of the three instinctual needs—survival and security, power and control, and affection and esteem—will tend to predominate. These have a certain value when pursued in moderation, but the advertising world and society in general are trying to get us to have more and more needs so that they can sell more and more of their stuff. Possessiveness is about the accumulation of things—a life that is about quantity not quality.

In any case, while this careful reader we've been talking about is assimilating the text, and the text is assimilating the reader; he or she may be turned on by something in the text and experience positive emotions. She doesn't change her concerns or her need of help, but now she begins to have a sense that there is something to help and that there is not just a big hole or a void or a hopeless situation. In other words, the Divine Indwelling (words in the Christian tradition) the Buddha Nature (from the Buddhist tradition), the Divine Spark (from the Hindu Vedanta tradition)—is beginning to vibrate. Why? Because it has always been there. It was just drowned out by habits of seeking satisfaction and happiness in the wrong places. We come to full reflective self-consciousness with an ego that has made itself the center of the world, around which everything else circulates like planets around the sun. Thus, when events or people enter our gravitational field, they are judged not on their objective goodness, but rather on whether they serve our particular emotional needs to find happiness in one or all of the three instinctual needs necessary for the infant, but most inappropriate for adult human beings. In early childhood these needs regularly become exaggerated, and hence impossible to realize. The use of reason is not yet present in the child to moderate them, so they fossilize into personality traits and programs for happiness that make demands on ourselves and on other people to fulfill our emotional needs, and thus not feel the pain of their frustration. And when we do, the ensuing emotional traumas are repressed into the unconscious to avoid the pain. The body is the warehouse in which the negative energies are stored. You can almost see them in some people or contact some of them in massage therapy.

TS: You mentioned massage. In your writings, you have observed that the body is the storehouse of "undigested emotions." Would you comment on that?

TK: A masseuse can feel pockets of grief, fear, panic, anger, or other emotions in our bodies that have never been processed and that are part of the emotional pain that give rise to the addictive process. The addictive process is the accumulation of frustration from failed emotional programs for happiness and the consequent afflictive emotions of anger, grief, fear, shame, guilt, depression, discouragement, and tormenting desires that are the consequences. The satisfaction of our emotional programs leads to elation, self-inflation, and pride. Both responses prevent us from relating to the Higher Power, ourselves, and other people in a way that is truly human. The process of divine intimacy engages our ordinary human faculties—even the body—in relationship with the Higher Power. Since we are made in the image of the Higher Power, we have within us as our basic core of goodness everything we need to be at peace and happy in the present moment. Only we don't know it because, like a diamond hidden under an enormous heap of garbage, the layers of false-self programs, thoroughly defended and increased by the traumas of our lives as they unfold, conceal God's presence within us.

TS: Would you tell us more about the last stage of this process or path to emotional stability?

TK: Actually, we're coming to the deepest part of this discussion—or to the place the three forms of preparation lead. Once again the four steps are listening to God speaking through the sacred text, reflecting with God about the text, and responding to God as a result of being moved by the text both emotionally and spiritually. These are preparations for something much more profound. The purpose of AA, as I understand it, is sobriety, recovery, and emotional stability—the words that you quoted from Bill W. at the beginning of our discussion. It is the fourth stage of the process of divine intimacy that opens us in the most comprehensive way to the experience that would bring about emotional stability, which is the discovery of where true happiness is to be found. This is called in Christian tradition, *resting in the presence of God*. Practically speaking, this happens gradually as those three stages of assimilating the text are pursued more or less daily at AA meetings and privately through periods of twenty-to-thirty minutes of the prayerful reading of a sacred text. In this context, prayer means developing a relationship with the Higher Power and a receptivity to the wisdom that is being offered in the particular text that we are trying to assimilate.

As this assimilating process continues, once in a while you may slip into the experience of your True Self. In other words, after having thought about an insight and responded with a certain depth of emotion, there comes a moment when you no longer want to read more or to repeat the same responses because you feel yourself called to a deeper place in which your response is not conversation or words, but communion with a Presence. That is called *contemplative prayer* in the Christian tradition. There are similar states of consciousness in other world religions.

What follows is a little difficult to grasp. I offer it for what it's worth. Some time in your development you identify with the Mystery and slip into *just being—just resting* in the Higher Power (God) in a disposition of receptivity, sensing the presence of the Mystery without any desire to articulate it or explain it to yourself. In other words, you move beyond reflection and your conceptual apparatus to an intuitive place where, ever so gently and gradually, or sometimes suddenly, you become aware that you are in union with the Mystery. The true "you" is a participation in the Divine Consciousness itself; hence, it is an experience of intimacy that is deeper than is possible with any human being. There is an interpenetration of spirits.

However, even in human love a similar experience arises at times. Think of an elderly couple for instance, who really love each other, sitting on the porch, watching the sunset or listening to music. They don't need to speak to each other to be happy because they have moved from talking to a permanent emotional exchange through the repeated gift of their presence to each other. What they are celebrating in silence is self-surrender—the gift of each to the other. And so, at least for the moment, they don't need words. It doesn't mean that they won't use them the rest of the evening, but these are kind of peak moments when they are aware that they are in touch with a higher communion, a higher presence, a higher love than they ordinarily experience in the everyday-life pressure of earning a living, rearing a family, and so on.

Thus, resting in God is the experience of loving and of being loved. It is an experience of just being present to each other with immense peace, contentment, and delight. This example of a couple's mature love is a lively symbol of what contemplative prayer actually is. It is a form of communing with God that awakens us to the deeper levels of happiness that are waiting for us, once we respond to the invitation to the deep knowledge and love of God.

TS: Would you comment further on the peak moment concept?

TK: Each one of those steps has certain peak moments, and then subsides. Thus, there is a dialogue between our activity and the inspiration that the Higher Power arouses within us. Sometimes the Divine Presence comes about not just gently but powerfully. That is why these first three stages need to be put in place as a necessary or at least very helpful preparation. The Divine Presence is always within us holding us in being at every moment—twenty-four hours a day. Creation is an ongoing and continuous act. The fact that we're sitting here is because God is holding us in being—body, soul, spirit—at every nanosecond of time.

With respect to this dialogue, there's a traditional Latin phrase that I referred to earlier. The Latin phrase goes like this: *mysterium tremendum et fascinans.* The common element between these two aspects is the Mystery of God's presence, that is to say, it is not something within the ordinary range of our knowledgeable faculties. It comes upon us as the result of this process of developing divine intimacy that we have just attempted to describe. At some point, the rest is not only restful and beyond concepts and words, but is overwhelming. In other words, there are moments of extreme wonder, awe, reverence, gratitude, attraction, and amazement, all wrapped into one. And if we do not have some preparation for it, it may be frightening.

Tremendum means overwhelming, enormous, inconceivable. It is like looking out on the universe nowadays. Here we are on the earth and our whole idea of ourselves has changed with the discovery of the galaxies moving away from the original starting point of the Big Bang at enormous speed. In another generation or two we won't even be able to see them because they are too far away for the light to get back to us, ever. So the universe, itself, is a *mysterium tremendum.* We can't imagine what it is. Wherever it is going, it is going at an ever-increasing speed.

In deep prayer we're confronted by the Mystery itself: by this hidden and secret Presence that has been within us all our life long, and which suddenly introduces itself—not through concepts or feelings, but as it actually is. This may be overwhelming for the human spirit when it first occurs. Yet, you do not want to run away because the other aspect is inherent in the very character of the overwhelming experience, and that is the *mysterium fascinans,* which is the fascination of the mystery and the irresistible attraction it evokes in us to penetrate it to its depths. In other words, there are two pulls going on. One is repelling, and the other is drawing, and they are both irresistible. It's a kind of double-bind, you might say. It is an experience in which you cannot say "Yes" or "No" to either possibility. All we can do is to surrender without judgment and let go of everything that you consider your own, and let God be God within us. That experience is contemplation in the fullest sense of the term. *Enlightenment* is the term in the Eastern religious traditions. It is the fruit of the previous stages in which our faculties, by assimilating the message of the text, are able to handle such a marvelous experience that is altogether both awesome and attractive. God, as the Higher Power, is so high that to experience this raw presence without the reassuring attraction of love could be mind blowing.

I remember a young man who came to our guesthouse at the monastery who had had such an experience without having been reared in any religious context. He didn't think of it as God. He just thought he was going crazy. For him the experience was unbearable. But as soon as he heard that God was present within him and that all he needed to do was to add the further dimension of God's caring and nurturing love, he found peace and reassurance.

TS: I think many of us could identify with that young man. At this point, could you give us a brief summary of this process of divine intimacy?

TK: The opening of divine intimacy can be done in various ways. One of the most traditional paths in all the traditions is sacred reading or, more exactly, listening with receptivity, respect, and complete attentiveness while engaged with the text. It consists also in a certain sensitivity to follow the attraction to reflect and not to rush on out of habit either by speed-reading or our usual way of dealing with literature, which is to read as fast as possible, pick out a few thoughts, and throw the rest away. No. It is a tendency to find in every sentence something worth mulling over, without exaggerating or mythologizing the value of any particular word or sentence. It is the general text that is communicating to us the wisdom that we need to receive at a deep level.

Reflecting on the text begins to undermine our facile pre-packaged values, preoccupations, and ideas of where we will find happiness based on the emotional programs for happiness of early childhood, that is, for the instinctual and prompt gratification of desires for power, affection, and security. Reflections on the text usually awaken desires for the good things we read about, such as hope of recovery, the healing of at least some of our relationships, or that we might begin to lead a life that is fully integrated into normal human society. All of these aspirations involve reactions that are powerful enough to transform our basic attitudes or habitual ways of acting.

Finally, when the emotions have subsided a bit and the thoughts have simplified into such simple words as, "I'm in peace," or "I feel grateful," then you let even those few words go and move into a loving silence, like the aging couple we referred to, who really loved each other and knew how to relish each other's presence. You begin to realize that this Higher Power loves you infinitely, is caring, motherly, and leading you through these stages of relationship to divine union. Negative feelings are not punishments for having acted in an irresponsible way, but ways of healing the deepest wounds of our lifetime. It's at that level that emotional sobriety becomes fully possible as a habitual way of life.

Experiences of the *mysterium tremendum et fascinans* may be few and far between, but they are life-changing. They give us the strength, honesty, and capacity to look at our lives and our weaknesses, brokenness, and the mess we sometimes have made of our relationships, without distress and with a certain contentment. Whatever we did wrong, we acknowledge that we did it, but we're not going to let it stand in the way of letting God heal us in whatever way He chooses. In other words, we're prepared to make amends.

The experience of God's love enables us to come to life in the fullest sense of the word and to lay aside, or at least relativize, those programs for happiness which, when gratification was withheld, led to a desperate need to get away from the pain of frustration and ensuing afflictive emotions. This is the addictive process that landed us eventually in some particular addiction, and which will land us in another addiction if we recover from alcohol, unless we attain emotional sobriety, through the deep knowledge of the Higher Power and our surrender to God's will in every aspect of our lives.

TS: One thing occurred to me when you used the Latin

term *mysterium tremendum*. Would the expression "spiritual awakening" mean the same thing in AA language?

TK: Yes, it would. Most people are not spiritually awakened. That's why they're looking for happiness in the wrong places, doing great injury to their relationships with the Higher Power, themselves, and other people. That's why the experience of God—even though awesome and overwhelming—is the ultimate source of true humility, which is to accept reality as it is. But we normally cannot do that until we have relativized our emotional expectations of what life can give us by way of happiness. Our cultural conditioning and all forms of institutions can offer us only external forms of happiness.

I venture to say that a merely external working of the Twelve Steps will not bring about this transformation either. Hence, as a practical point, prayerful and attentive reading of the traditional texts of AA and impressing upon AA members the importance of the assimilation of the wisdom of the founders, is crucial for achieving emotional sobriety, which is the most certain support for recovery, insofar as that is possible in this world.

TS: So, what you are describing today is really a pathway to a spiritual awakening.

TK: That's exactly what it is. This is also my understanding of what the Twelve Step program is.

TS: As you know, over the past twenty years I have used the method of "centering prayer" as my eleventh step meditation. Would you comment on how centering prayer could be used as the fourth stage of the awakening process?

TK: Centering prayer emphasizes resting in God or the final stage of the process of Lectio Divina. Resting in God can be accessed directly without passing through these preliminary steps that we call Lectio Divina. It consists in simply being in the presence of God and deliberately letting go of other thoughts, even thoughts about God. In other words, for the time being we've moved into a graced moment of intimacy in which the experience of being and of self-surrender is paramount rather than the intermediary of words, feelings, and thoughts. It is another way of accessing the *mysterium tremendum et fascinans*, but without the intermediary of preliminary steps.

The centering prayer practice could be appropriately considered for those who had an attraction to it at the sixth or seventh step of the AA path to awakening. The sixth step, as I understand it, is "We became willing that God would take away our faults." Following the personal inventory and sharing one's whole life of misdemeanors with a sponsor, the next step, as we saw, would seem to be to do something about one's behavior and try to correct these faults. But that isn't the sixth step. Even to pray to be delivered only comes in the seventh step! This is a striking insight that is also prominent in the Christian path, which alerts us to the fact that we do not accomplish this process ourselves. By trying, we find out that our efforts do not work, and that the only thing that can heal us is to give ourselves over entirely to the Higher Power: God in the Christian tradition.

Through the practice of interior silence we are invited to look into the depths of our motivation. Here is where centering prayer would add to "the depths of our unconscious motivation," because centering prayer by resting in God and by the consent to the attraction of silence, opens our ordinary psychological awareness to the spiritual level of our nature—the level of intuition and the spiritual will. This level of interior silence makes us vulnerable to the contents of the unconscious. I venture to say that it is the content of our unconscious that is the source of everybody's problems to begin with, whether they are members of AA or not. According to Bill W., members of AA often fall into a depression after ten years of sobriety. I suggest that this may be because they have not yet discovered their real motivation, which is still hidden in their unconscious. The centering prayer practice makes us vulnerable to the unconscious, especially after we have established a certain intimacy and at-easeness with God through the first three movements of Lectio Divina—reading, reflecting, responding. Now we are strong enough and humble enough to allow our selfish motivation and childish ways of acting to come to consciousness. Naturally, this is uncomfortable in the beginning, but the regular practice of resting in God also involves the affirmation of our basic goodness. Thus we're able to balance the negative awareness of our shadow side, as Jung calls it—the personality traits that are driving our friends up the wall and making our lives unmanageable—with the positive goodness that is beginning to emerge from the fact that we are also the image of God.

Centering prayer could be a strong ally of the Twelve Steps for those who can connect with it or who might be attracted to it. It is already being used by some members of the Twelve Step groups as a particular method for the eleventh step. It might be helpful at an earlier step in AA and perhaps hasten the process of recovery. If we allow the Divine Indwelling or the Higher Power to heal the wounds of our unconscious, the addictive process will end and there will be no more addictions. There will still be preferences. There will be feelings of distress. But they will not touch the deep peace or calm that the Psalms refer to as the rock on which we are based, the God in whom we confidently take refuge. Awakening to the Divine Indwelling is the true security, the true freedom, and the true love of our lives.

TS: That is a great observation. And I particularly agree with regard to the sixth step. During the first five steps most of us are working on our ordinary levels of spiritual awareness, and we're just not ready for the deep exposure of our unconscious motivations. But maybe in the sixth step, to some degree, we could start the process of a deeper healing.

TK: The sixth step, it seems to me, presupposes that you do not know your faults or the depth of your attachments to them, or the amount of energy you put into your emotional programs for happiness. It is all unconscious. You need a practice that exposes you to the unconscious if the full meaning of the sixth step is to emerge. We rather like our faults, and we don't even know that we do because our attachment is also in the unconscious. The sixth step presupposes that we have moved far enough to be willing, as our faults emerge, to have them taken away. If we were willing, God would take them away immediately. Moreover, you have to be willing before you pray to have them taken away; otherwise, you would be hypocritical, asking for something you don't really want.

TS: My observation is that people who have taken the Twelve Steps and who have been in AA for a few years, will often move back to the sixth step to review it because their sponsor recognizes that some of their ingrained character defects are still in control. My sense is, if they went back to the sixth step and incorporated the practice of centering prayer, they might be able to go to that deeper level that will give them the healing they need.

I would like to thank you for this interview, Father. You've covered the topics so well. I think there is a huge need within AA for experiencing the steps in depth and maybe structuring step meetings or our private readings so that they could lead us to an in-depth absorption of the principles they represent. It seems that the measure of this absorption has always been the key to emotional sobriety for many alcoholics.

Our interview this weekend, with God's help, may be

the starting point for a new spiritual awareness within the Twelve Step community.

TK: If there is some value in this process of learning how to read as listening so that the wisdom of one's tradition is truly assimilated and interiorized, then it would seem to me that instruction in how to do this would be part of the fundamental teaching of AA. Once people come to the meeting, they need to hear this fairly soon so that they can really absorb what they are reading.

TS: Perhaps a workshop of some kind. . . .

TK: Or at least special training for sponsors so that many of them could impart this material privately. Since so many groups are ongoing, you don't want to hear the same thing over and over again, or really need to. But some practical way of communicating how to make the best use of the treasures of the Twelve Steps and the Twelve Traditions might enable more people to persevere in the difficult starting-out years.

TS: And stay alive. . . .

APPENDIX A

The Next Frontier: Emotional Sobriety,
Bill W., January 1958

I think that many oldsters who have put our AA "booze cure" to severe but successful tests still find they often lack emotional sobriety. Perhaps they will be the spearhead for the next major development in AA—the development of much more real maturity and balance (which is to say, humility) in our relations with ourselves, with our fellows, and with God.

Those adolescent urges that so many of us have for top approval, perfect security, and perfect romance urges quite appropriate to a seventeen-year-old prove to be an impossible way of life when we are forty-seven or fifty-seven.

Since AA began, I have taken immense wallops in all these areas because of my failure to grow up, emotionally and spiritually. My God, how hard it is to keep demanding the impossible, and how very painful to discover finally, that all along we have had the cart before the horse! Then comes the final agony of seeing how awfully wrong we have been, but still finding ourselves unable to get off the emotional merry-go-round.

How to translate a right mental conviction into a right emotional result, and so into easy, happy, and good living—

well, that is not only the neurotic's problem, it is the problem of life itself for all of us who have got to the point of real willingness to hew to right principles in all our affairs.

Even then, as we hew away, peace and joy may still elude us. That's the place so many of us AA oldsters have come to. And it's a hell of a spot, literally. How shall our unconscious, from which so many of our fears, compulsions, and phony aspirations still stream, be brought into line with what we actually believe, know, and want? How to persuade our dumb, raging, and hidden "Mr. Hyde" becomes our main task.

I have recently come to believe that this can be achieved. I believe so because I begin to see many benighted ones, folks like you and me, commencing to get results. Last autumn, depression, having no really rational cause at all, almost took me to the cleaners. I began to be scared that I was in for another long chronic spell. Considering the grief I've had with depressions, it wasn't a bright prospect.

I kept asking myself, "Why can't the Twelve Steps work to release depression?" By the hour, I stared at the St. Francis prayer . . . "It's better to comfort than to be comforted." Here was the formula, all right. But why didn't it work?

Suddenly, I realized what the matter was. My basic flaw had always been dependence, almost absolute dependence, on people or circumstances to supply me with prestige, security, and the like. Failing to get these things according to my perfectionist dreams and specifications, I had fought for them. And when defeat came, so did my depression.

There wasn't a chance of making the outgoing love of St. Francis a workable and joyous way of life until these fatal and almost absolute dependencies were cut away.

Because I had over the years undergone a little spiritual development, the *absolute* quality of these frightful dependencies had never before been so starkly revealed. Reinforced by what grace I could secure in prayer, I found I had to exert every ounce of will and action to cut off these faulty emotional dependencies upon people in AA, indeed, upon any set of circumstances whatsoever. Only then could I be free to love as Francis had. Emotional and instinctual satisfactions, I saw, were really the extra dividends of having love, offering love, and expressing a love appropriate to each relation of life.

Plainly, I could not avail myself of God's love until I was able to offer it back to Him by loving others as He would have me. And I couldn't possibly do that so long as I was victimized by false dependencies.

For my dependency meant demand—a demand for the possession and control of the people and the conditions surrounding me.

While those words "absolute dependency" may look like a gimmick, they were the ones that helped to trigger my release into my present degree of stability and quietness of mind, qualities which I am now trying to consolidate by offering love to others regardless of the return to me.

This seems to be the primary healing circuit: an outgoing love of God's creation and his people, by means of which we avail ourselves of his love for us. It is most clear that the real current can't flow until our paralyzing dependencies are broken, and broken at depth. Only then can we possibly have a glimmer of what love really is.

Spiritual calculus, you say? Not a bit of it. Watch any AA of six months working with a new twelfth step case. If the case says, "To the devil with you," the Twelfth Stepper only smiles and turns to another case. He doesn't feel frustrated or rejected. If his next case responds, and in turn starts to give love and attention to other alcoholics, yet gives none back to him, the sponsor is happy about it anyway. He still doesn't feel rejected. Instead, he rejoices that his one-time prospect is sober and happy. And if his following case turns out in later times to be his best friend (or romance), then the sponsor is most joyful. But he well knows that his happiness is a by-product, the extra dividend of giving without any demand for a return.

The really stabilizing thing for him was having and offering love to that strange drunk on his doorstep. That was Francis at work, powerful and practical, minus dependency and minus demand.

In the first six months of my own sobriety, I worked hard with many alcoholics. Not a one responded. Yet this work kept me sober. It wasn't a question of those alcoholics giving me anything. My stability came out of trying to give, not out of demanding that I receive.

Thus, I think it can work out with emotional sobriety. If we examine every disturbance we have, great or small, we will find at the root of it some unhealthy dependency and its consequent unhealthy demand. Let us, with God's help, continuously surrender these hobbling demands. Then we can be set free to live and love; we may then be able to twelfth step ourselves and others into emotional sobriety.

Of course I haven't offered you a really new idea, only a gimmick that has started to unhook several of my own "hexes" at depth. Nowadays my brain no longer races compulsively in either elation, grandiosity, or depression. I have been given a quiet place in bright sunshine.

APPENDIX B

An Eleventh Step Prayer Practice
for those in Twelve Step Programs

THE METHOD OF CENTERING PRAYER

Sought through prayer and meditation to improve our conscious contact with God as we understood Him.

This pamphlet was put together to help those searching for emotional and spiritual sobriety. Centering prayer is a method for doing the eleventh step to improve our conscious contact with our Higher Power. "Sought through prayer and meditation" deals with our own personal effort to communicate with a Higher Power. Many people in Twelve Step Programs have deepened their relationship with their Higher Power with the method of centering prayer. This is about you and your God "as you understand God." It is not an attempt to change the instructions given in the Big Book, but to support and supplement them.

A NEW FREEDOM

Whether you have been in recovery for a long time or are just beginning, you probably have experienced a lot of frustrated feelings that didn't just go away when you got abstinent or sober . . . problems with relationships, work, anxiety, depression, or feelings of emptiness. These feelings are natural for us no matter what our addiction and the amount of time in recovery we have. But we don't have to let them rule our lives. The eleventh step offers us a solution!

Through the simple method of centering prayer we can improve our relationship with the Ultimate Power of life. This is true whether we call the power God, Allah, Mother, another name, or no name.

This type of prayer has been used over the centuries, but it is different from what we may think of as prayer. It is not the type of prayer we are used to, like prayer for something we want. It is simply moving deep within ourselves, in silence saying nothing, asking for nothing, just being and allowing our Higher Power to be with us.

For those who are working a recovery program, parallels can be found between the transformation that centering prayer brings and the process of growth facilitated as we work the Twelve Steps.

SOME PRACTICAL POINTS

1. Twenty minutes of centering prayer twice a day is recommended.

2. If you notice slight physical or emotional pain arising during the prayer, pay no attention and return ever so gently to the sacred word.

3. It is suggested that you join a weekly centering prayer group to find others in recovery, willing to meet on a regular basis, to support one another in this practice.

ABOUT TWELVE STEP OUTREACH

Many people are already practicing centering prayer and find it very helpful to their recovery. Twelve Step Outreach offers retreats and introductory workshops that teach this method in more depth.

You can find information about workshops and retreats offered by the Twelve Step Outreach at *www.contemplativeoutreach.org* and click on "programs."

THE GUIDELINES

1. Choose a sacred word as the symbol of your intention to consent to God's presence and action within.

2. Sitting comfortably with eyes closed, settle briefly, and silently introduce the sacred word as the symbol of your consent to God's presence and action within.

3. When engaged with your thoughts, return ever so gently to the sacred word.

4. At the end of the prayer period, remain in silence with eyes closed for a couple of minutes.

The "sacred word" is sacred not because of its inherent meaning, but because of the meaning we give it as the expression of our intention and consent. Examples: *Love,*

Let Go, Serenity, Peace, Silence, Faith, Trust, Gentle, and so forth.

"Sitting comfortably" means relatively comfortably so as not to encourage sleep during the time of prayer.

Thoughts include body sensations, feelings, images, and reflections. By "returning ever-so-gently to the sacred word" a minimum of effort is indicated. This is the only activity we initiate during the time of centering prayer.

EFFECTS OF CENTERING PRAYER

The effects of the prayer are experienced in daily life and not necessarily during the prayer period itself. During this prayer, avoid analyzing the experience, or having expectations such as: continuously repeating the sacred word; having no thoughts; achieving a spiritual experience. It is important not to judge the success of your prayer period. The only thing you can do wrong in this prayer is to get up and leave. You may find yourself getting in touch with feelings of pain, lust, or fear, even remembering feelings or events you forgot about long ago. There is no way to change or repair the damage of a lifetime easily and quickly.

Everyone moves at his or her own pace in centering prayer. Just doing the prayer and opening oneself to the presence of the Higher Power in silence encourages us to keep going.

Growth will happen when we practice centering prayer in the context of the Twelve Steps:

- Enhances our ability to "Let Go and Let God"
- Develops in us a nonjudgmental attitude of ourselves and others
- We grow in self-knowledge, which at times might be painful
- Emerging capacity to listen and serve others
- Nurtures our ability to live in the present moment and just for today

ABOUT CENTERING PRAYER

Thomas Keating, OCSO, is one of the founders of the centering prayer movement and Contemplative Outreach, a spiritual network that teaches centering prayer and provides a support system for those who practice it. He is the author of many books and recorded presentations on contemplative prayer.

In 2001, the Twelve Step Outreach Program of Contemplative Outreach was established to offer centering prayer to people in all Twelve Step fellowships as an eleventh step prayer/meditation practice. We help individuals and groups establish contemplative prayer practices through workshops, retreats, and formation programs.

The practice of centering prayer, and the spiritual, historical, and psychological basis of it, are described and elaborated in several of Thomas Keating's works, including *Open Mind, Open Heart,* and *Invitation to Love.* The practice of centering prayer has parallels with other traditional practices, and is simple and easy to do.

For those who live by the Twelve Steps found in AA, Al-Anon, SCA, OA, DA, NA, GA, and other programs, a centering prayer practice can be a key support system in the process of recovery and transformation.

Centering prayer can help deepen our application of the Twelve Steps generally, and the eleventh step specifically, through daily immersion in prayer and meditation. We believe that, when applied as a daily supplement to the Twelve Steps, centering prayer opens us to the deepest dimension of spirituality.

APPENDIX C

Listing of the Twelve Steps

1. We admitted that we were powerless over alcohol, that our lives had become unmanageable.

2. Came to believe that a power greater than ourselves could restore us to sanity.

3. Made a decision to turn our will and our lives over to the care of God as we understood Him.

4. Made a searching and fearless moral inventory of ourselves.

5. Admitted to God, to ourselves, and to another human being the exact nature of our wrongs .

6. Were entirely ready to have God remove all these defects of character.

7. Humbly asked Him to remove our shortcomings.

8. Made a list of all persons we had harmed, and became willing to make amends to them all.

9. Made direct amends to such people wherever possible, except when to do so would injure them or others.

10. Continued to take personal inventory and when we were wrong, promptly admitted it

11. Sought through prayer and meditation to improve our conscious contact with God as we understood Him, praying only for knowledge of His will for us and the power to carry that out.

12. Having had a spiritual awakening as the result of these steps, we tried to carry this message to alcoholics and to practice these principles in all our affairs.

Tax-deductible grants to further this work can be sent to: Tom S., c/o Contemplative Outreach, Ltd., 10 Park Place, 2nd Floor, Suite 2B, Butler, New Jersey 07405—payable to Contemplative Outreach, Ltd.—for the "Tom S. Grant Account" (covers expenses only, all work is voluntary).

DVDs of some of the interviews are available.

Titles by, on, or featuring Thomas Keating
from Lantern Books

Natanel Miles-Yepez, Editor
The Common Heart
An Experience of Interreligious Dialogue
144 pp, 978-1-59056-099-X

The Divine Indwelling
Centering Prayer and Its Development
112 pp, 978-1-930051-79-9

Fruits and Gifts of the Spirit
128 pp, 978-1-930051-21-8

Manifesting God
144 pp, 978-1-59056-85-X

St. Thérèse of Lisieux
A Transformation in Christ
96 pp, 978-1-930051-20-4

The Transformation of Suffering
*Reflections on September 11
and the Wedding Feast at Cana in Galilee*
64 pp, 978-1-59056-036-1

Spirituality, Contemplation, and Transformation
Writings on Centering Prayer
348 pp, 978-1-59056-110-2

Sundays at the Magic Monastery
Homilies from the Trappists of St. Benedict's Monastery
144 pp, 978-1-59056-033-7

Fr. Murchadh O Madagain
**Centering Prayer and
the Healing of the Unconscious**
336 pp, 978-1-59056-107-2